Incarnational Spirituality

Embodying the Love of the Incarnate Word

Adaku H. Ogbuji, CCVI, PhD (Editor)

En Route Books and Media, LLC
Saint Louis, MO

En Route Books and Media, LLC
5705 Rhodes Avenue
St. Louis, MO 63109

Contact us at **contact@enroutebooksandmedia.com**

Cover Credit: Adaku H. Ogbuji, CCVI, PhD
© 2023 Adaku H. Ogbuji, CCVI, PhD (Editor)

ISBN-13: 979-8-88870-115-7
Library of Congress Control Number: 2023952031

First Published in 2022 by Franciscan Kolbe Press, P.O. Box 468, Nairobi, Kenya. Republished with the author's permission in 2023 by En Route Books & Media, LLC.

All rights reserved. No part of this book may be reproduced, stored in a retrieval system, or transmitted in any form or by any means electronic, mechanical, photocopying, recording or otherwise, without the prior written permission of the copyright owner.

Dedication

This reflection is dedicated to Sr. Susanne Ruane, CCVI, who inspired and encouraged the writing of this book, and to all Religious Congregations, especially the Congregation of the Sisters of Charity of the Incarnate Word, who live Incarnational Spirituality.

Table of Contents

Introduction by Sr. Adaku H. Ogbuji, CCVI 1

Chapter 1: Incarnational Spirituality by Sr. Adaku H. Ogbuji, CCVI 5

Chapter 2: Praying the Angelus with a Humanized God in a Dehumanized World by Sr. Adaku H. Ogbuji, CCVI 17

Chapter 3: Incarnational Spirituality: The Spirituality of Compassion by Sr. Adaku H. Ogbuji, CCVI 29

Chapter 4: Incarnational Spirituality and the Care of Creation by Sr. Margret Bulmer, CCVI 43

Chapter 5: Incarnational Spirituality and Forgiveness by Sr. Adaku H. Ogbuji, CCVI 53

Chapter 6: Incarnational Spirituality and Religious Community Living by Sr. Patience S. Payne, S.H.F 65

Chapter 7: Embodying the Love of the Incarnate Word in Intercultural and Intergenerational Religious Communities by Sr. Adaku H. Ogbuji, CCVI 73

Chapter 8: Attitudes and Dispositions for Incarnational Formative Process by Fr. Remigius Ikpe (O.C.D.) 95

Chapter 9: Embodying The Love of the Incarnate Word in Mission by Sr. Adaku H. Ogbuji, CCVI 111

Chapter 10: Embodying the Love of the Incarnate Word by Sr. Adaku H. Ogbuji, CCVI 127

References 135

About the Contributors 139

Introduction

Sr. Adaku H. Ogbuji, CCVI

On June 1, 2021, I received an email from Sr. Susanne Ruane, CCVI, in which she wrote: "Sr. Helena, I love your article on the Angelus. I would encourage you to write a book on incarnational spirituality for our Congregation. You are blessed with the gift of writing and insight, and it would be a wonderful gift to the Congregation. Thank you and God's blessing. Sr. Susanne."

After reading her email, I was filled with excitement and responded: "Thank you so much Sr. Susanne for instilling this insight in me. I have started thinking about a book on incarnational spirituality already. God willing, I will dedicate the book to you. Pray for me that God will give me insights and wisdom. Thank you, Sr. Susanne. You are in my prayers, too. With love, Helena." This short encounter gave rise to the book in your hands.

From the moment I read and answered Sr. Susanne's email, I began to imagine and reflect on what authentic incarnational spirituality could mean in our broken world and how embodying the love of the Incarnate Word could heal our wounded society. The picture was not clear, so I reread some excerpts from our Constitutions:

> As Sisters of Charity of the Incarnate Word, we are sent to embody God's love through our apostolic religious community. We place our individual and communal gifts at the

service of Christ and his Church. (Mission and Ministry, Article 43)

Entrusted as we are with the mission of embodying the love of the Incarnate Word, we bear in mind that, whatever the form of our ministry, it is by means of our own lives that we witness most convincingly to the presence of Jesus Christ. (Mission and Ministry, Article 47)

As I reflected on these beautiful words from Our Way of Life, I also read our Directives to try to comprehend what I was reflecting on:

In relationships among ourselves, with our co-workers, and those to whom we minister, we try to be patient, gentle and compassionate. (Directives 47.1)

Embodying the love of the Incarnate Word is not lived out in a vacuum. It has consequences! It is connected with the three questions Jesus asked Peter after his resurrection: "Peter, do you love me?" Of course, Peter loved the Lord, but Jesus needed Peter to confess his love for him, which comes with some demands. "If you love me, feed/tend my sheep." Loving God does not add anything to God's greatness; however, God still wants us to love Him and have a relationship with Him. It is this relationship with God that we extend to the people around us. This is because we cannot claim to love God whom we have not seen if we don't have love for our neighbours (1 Jn.4:20).

Introduction

In reflecting on the meaning of embodying the love of the Incarnate Word, I was also wondering how enlightening, extensive, and wide-ranging this book would be if there were other intelligent contributors to the work. I reached out to some CCVI Sisters and to religious outside of my Congregation. Many of my sisters would have loved to contribute by writing a chapter or two but, unfortunately, they were very busy.

Happily, I got three additional contributors to this work. I want to thank Sister Margaret Bulmer, CCVI, for sparing her time to expand, very intelligently, on the connection between incarnational spirituality and the care of creation in chapter four. I also thank my friends Sr. Patience Payne and Fr. Remigius Ikpe for helping to make this book enlightening with their wonderful insights in chapters six and eight respectfully. In our reflections, we expounded on these questions: What does it mean to embody the love of the Incarnate Word, at this time, in our religious communities and in the whole world? Where is God sending us today to embody this love? What gifts are we bringing and placing at the service of Christ and His Church? The answers to these and more questions will be considered in this reflection.

The book is divided into ten chapters. In the first chapter, I reflect on the meaning of incarnational spirituality, and in chapter two, discuss the mystery of the humanized God in a dehumanized world. In chapter three, I continue to reflect on incarnational spirituality as the spirituality of compassion. Sr. Margret Bulmer, CCVI, illuminates how incarnational spirituality and the care of creation are connected in chapter four, while I reflect on the connection between incarnational spirituality and forgiveness in chapter five. In chapter six, Sr. Patience Payne (HFS) explores how incarnational spirituality is important in our community living, while I expound on the importance of incarnational spirituality in our intercultural and intergenerational religious communities in chapter seven. Fr. Remigius Ikpe (O.C.D.), in chapter eight, explains the attitudes and dispositions formators should have if candidates in formation are to experience an incarnational formation process. In chapter nine, I reflect on how we embody the love of the Incarnate Word in Mission, and I conclude the work in chapter ten by reflecting on what it means to individually "Embody the Love of the Incarnate Word."

In putting our thoughts and reflections together, we do not claim to be experts in incarnational spirituality. However, we pray that it will help you in building a deeper relationship with the Incarnate Word, who became human so that we may become divine, and who modelled for us what being human truly is.

Chapter 1

Incarnational Spirituality

Sr. Adaku H. Ogbuji, CCVI

What is Incarnational Spirituality?

How much does it cost God to love you? To answer this question, look at the mystery of the Incarnation and of the cross. Flip the coin! How much does it cost you to love God? In other words, how much do you value your love for God and others? God is infinitely in love with us! God demonstrated this inconceivable and enormous love by sending Jesus, the Incarnate Word, who, while we were still sinners, not only became human but also died for us (Rm. 5:8). It is this infinite, boundless, and immeasurable love of God that is reflected in the mystery of Incarnation. Before we reflect on this mystery, it is necessary to explain what spirituality is.

Once I asked a group of formatees: what is spirituality? Some said it is living spiritually, while a few said it is having faith in God, and still others defined it as having a relationship with God. All these responses are not far from the truth. However, spirituality is not only about being a Christian since even atheists are spiritual beings and have spirituality. Spirituality is about being human. It is who we are—embodied spiritual beings. On the other hand, devotion to God or having a relationship with Him, are a part of being a spiritual being. It is a spiritual devotion that connects one with God, through faith, and leads to holiness.

In his famous book *The Holy Longing: The Search for a Christian Spirituality,* Ronald Rolheiser explains that spirituality is the energy within us that drives us to do good or evil. Everyone has this energy. Our humanness is accompanied by this energy that burns like a fire within us. This energy drives us to do good works of charity, loving all humanity, as well as deterring us from causing harm or any other evil. This fiery desire that burns within can be channelled into life-giving activities or used for destructive purposes. For Rolheiser, "spirituality is how we handle the fire of desire that burns within us." We can channel this fire into becoming more like the healing presence of Jesus in our communities or ministries, by serving with gladness those that we are called to serve, and in embodying the love of the Incarnate Word in our everyday activities. On the other hand, we can channel this energy into destructive habits such as gossiping, hatred, prejudice, racism, unforgiveness, and other negative attitudes. The ball is in our court! It is up to us to decide how we want to handle our individual energies.

Every human is a spiritual being, first by virtue of being created by God, and second by the mystery of the incarnation. By virtue of being created in the image and likeness of God, we are spiritual beings. The Psalmist says: "You are gods, and all of you are children of the Most High" (Ps. 82:6). In another verse, the Psalmist reiterated: "Yet you have made them a little lower than God,

Chapter 1: Incarnational Spirituality

and crowned them with glory and honour" (Ps. 8:5). Jesus also refers to us as embodied spiritual beings when he answered the people, "Is it not written in your Law, 'I said, you are gods'?" (Jn. 10:34).

Furthermore, we are spiritual beings by virtue of the mystery of the incarnation. Incarnation literally means embodied in flesh or taking on flesh. The conception of Jesus in the womb of Mary was not through natural or biological means. His conception was through the power of the Holy Spirit and is referred to as Incarnation. At the appointed time, God sent his Son, born of a woman, born under the law, to redeem those who were under the law so that we might receive adoption as children. And because you are children, God has sent the Spirit of his Son into our hearts, crying, "Abba! Father!" So, you are no longer a slave but a child, and if a child then also an heir, through God. (Gal. 4:4-7). St. Athanasius, Bishop of Alexandria (c. 296–373), stated: "The Word was made flesh in order that we might be made gods. Just as the Lord, putting on the body, became a man, so also, we are both deified through his flesh, and henceforth inherit everlasting life. For the Son of God became man so that we might become gods."

The mystery of the Incarnation is the ultimate value and expression of the love of God for us. It baffles me beyond words how God entrusted his life in the hands of two human beings—Mary and Joseph. God knew that human beings have the free will to do evil or to do good! Did God even imagine or consider the consequences of his decision to entrust his life in the care of humans? It gives me goosebumps when I reflect on this great mystery and God's immense love for humans. The Second Person of the Trinity and the Word of God emptied himself and became flesh (Phil. 2:7; Jn.1:14).

Out of love for humanity, Jesus became what we are—human; so that we might become what He is—Divine. In becoming flesh, Jesus was helpless and depended completely on the hands of his parents to care for him as a child. Imagine God tasting our developmental cycle! That is what LOVE does! Jesus also tasted our pain, our weakness, and our vulnerability with the exception of sin. Jesus was born human, so that we will be born again and in Spirit, through our baptism. Jesus explained this mystery when Nicodemus asked, "How can anyone be born after having grown old? Can one enter a second time into the mother's womb and be born?" Jesus answered, "Very truly, I tell you, no one can enter the kingdom of God without being born of water and Spirit. What is born of the flesh is flesh, and what is born of the Spirit is spirit." (Jn. 3:4-6).

Incarnational spirituality is therefore having a relationship with the God who became one of us and whose life mirrors how to be in a relationship with each other. It is a relational spirituality. It is not enough to say: "I am a follower of Christ," or "I am a priest/religious." We have to demonstrate our Christian life by embodying the love of the Incarnate Word and by living out the qualities of being human and being divine. These qualities are compassion, kind-heartedness, love, unselfishness, open-mindedness, empathy, forgiveness, benevolence, generosity, mercy, etc., just as our Creator, who made us "little less than gods." The prayer a priest says quietly when dropping water in the wine during Mass at the preparation of the gifts opines this truth: "By the mystery of the water in wine, may we come to share in the divinity of Christ who humbled himself to share in our humanity." We are very fortunate to share these qualities with Christ in his humanity and in his divinity. However, this good-nature of humanity was corrupted by sin after the fall, hence our humane qualities were corrupted and we exhibit and are lured into all sorts of wickedness and evil. Nevertheless, Jesus had to take flesh to exemplify what it means to be human.

The Fall and Its Impacts on our Incarnational Life

After the fall in Genesis 3:1-24, God planned to redeem humanity from its fallen nature. It was not the intention of God for humans, whom He created in His likeness, to sin. But when humans gave in to sin, God desired to redeem those lovely creatures of His. God first tested Abraham and talked him into sacrificing his only son Isaac. Although Abraham was willing to sacrifice Isaac, God intervened in time and provided a lamb for Sacrifice. However, at the appointed time, God's only Son, the sacrificial Lamb, would be sacrificed in place of Isaac. But before that sacrifice, God's Son—Jesus Christ—had to become human. He had to leave his throne in heaven and be born like us. This led to the mystery of the Incarnation.

St. John tells us that: "In the beginning was the Word, and the Word was with God, and the Word was God" (Jn. 1:1). By the power of the Holy Spirit, this Word was conceived in the womb of a woman, the Virgin Mary, and he became Emmanuel—God with us. This automatically made Jesus our brother. In the past, I was more comfortable relating to Jesus as a friend, Lord, or Saviour. However, seeing Jesus as my brother is a gift that I have recently been blessed to receive.

One day, I attended Mass at the Cathedral Basilica of St. Louis, Missouri. Rev. Msgr. Gregory R. Mikesch was celebrating the Mass, and his homily concerned the notion of "Jesus as our brother." He used the Easter scene where Jesus appeared to Mary Magdalene and sent her on an errand: "Go and tell my brothers, I am ascending to my Father and your Father, to my God and your God" (Jn.20:17). Msgr. Greg confessed that he also had not been comfortable addressing Jesus as a brother. So, he told his spiritual director during a thirty-day retreat: "I am comfortable to address Jesus as Lord, Messiah, Master or God, but it is very difficult to see him as a brother." The spiritual director told him: "Go talk to Jesus." In his prayer, he told Jesus: "You know I find it difficult to relate to you as a brother. I am more comfortable with Messiah, Lord, Master." Jesus asked him, "When I taught you how to pray, how did I begin?" He responded: "You began with 'Our Father.'" So, if I address God as Father and you also address Him as Father, what does it make us?" Msgr Greg responded: "I get it. We are siblings!"

From that moment, my relationship with Jesus deepened and became more intimate, similar to how I relate to my male siblings. Relating with Jesus as a sibling or a brother brings us closer to him, and we become more human as he was. Jesus is our brother because of the mystery of the Incarnation. He wants us to be in a relationship with his Father. By virtue of Jesus becoming flesh at the appointed time and through our baptism, we are children of

Chapter 1: Incarnational Spirituality

God and can address God as Abba just as Jesus did. In praying the Lord's Prayer, we are exercising our rights as children of the Father in heaven and connecting with our brother—Jesus Christ.

St. Paul writes: "But when the fullness of time had come, God sent his Son, born of a woman" (Gal. 4:4-7). With this passage, St. Paul threw more light on the mystery of the incarnation. This mystery is celebrated yearly during the feast of Annunciation but is fully commemorated each year at Christmas. The feast of annunciation is depicted in the Angelus prayer that we pray daily as Christians.

Just like us, Jesus was a true human with real human feelings. He laughed, cried, showed anger and frustration, and had good days as well as some bad ones, like when he cursed a fig tree because he could not eat from its fruit (Mk. 11:12-25). The poor tree was only obeying God's will for it, waiting for the right time to bear fruit. But Jesus was really hungry and desired food! He was human, too! In the same way, we experience good days and bad days, moments of anxiety, depression, and guilt. We are distracted, frustrated, and sometimes doubt our own abilities. We grieve and mourn, and we also celebrate joyfully and with excitement. Sometimes we are generous, compassionate, patient, and forgiving. Other times we are unkind and impatient. We discern what is good and what is evil, and we choose between them. Sometimes, we make wonderful decisions; other times, we choose the wrong path. We believe that God loves us, yet at times we doubt His love. Sometimes, we pray; other times, we experience dryness, emptiness, or absence of God and cannot pray. All these are part of being human and part of being an incarnational person.

When we experience God's absence or even doubt his existence, we ought to know that it is part of the spiritual journey. We are not going to enjoy only the consolation of God without seeking, in our aridity and desolation, the God who consoles us. Sometimes, we bask in the gift we have received, in this case, consolation, rather than in the Giver. The daily and important question to ask ourselves is whether we seek the consolation of God, or the God of consolation. We are not human beings having spiritual experiences; rather, we are spiritual beings having human experiences, says Teilhard de Chardin, SJ. And part of these human experiences are the joys and consolations of life as well as the struggles of life and our daily crosses.

The struggles and crosses we experience in our spiritual journeys are needed to help us purify our longings. They are necessary for our spiritual growth. This spiritual struggle reminds me of a story about a butterfly:

> One day a man found the cocoon of a butterfly and noticed that it had a small opening on one side. He sat and watched the butterfly for several hours as it struggled to force its body through the little hole. Then it seemed to stop making any progress. It appeared as if it had gotten as far as it could and could go no further. The man decided to help the butterfly, so he took a pair of scissors and carefully snipped the remaining bit of the cocoon. The butterfly then emerged easily, but something was strange. The butterfly had a swollen body and shrivelled wings. The man continued to watch the butterfly because he expected that at any

moment, the wings would enlarge and expand to be able to support the body, which would contract in time. Neither happened. In fact, the butterfly spent the rest of its life crawling around with a swollen body and deformed wings. It was never able to fly.

>Unknown author (Motivational Stories)

What the man, in his kindness, did not understand is that the restricting cocoon and the struggle required for the butterfly to get through the small opening of the cocoon is God's way of forcing fluid from the body of the butterfly into its wings so that it can be ready for flight once it achieves its freedom from the cocoon. At times, our struggles are exactly what we need in life, and they are what keeps us steadfast and unwavering in our journey of faith.

It is unfortunate that sometimes we tend to lose hope when we experience the absence of God during our dark moments. An atheist was once asked what he would say to God if he was to discover upon his death that God exists. He responded: "I would ask, 'Why did you hide?'" This is also depicted in the Psalmist's cry to God for help:

> Rouse yourself! Why do you sleep, O Lord?
> Awake, do not cast us off forever!
> Why do you hide your face?
> Why do you forget our affliction and oppression?
>   (Ps. 44:23-24)

God is not absent during our spiritual dryness or struggles. He is actually carrying us in his arms. This reality brings to my mind the popular poem about the "Footprints in the Sand" written by Mary Stevenson in 1939.

> One night I dreamed I was walking along the beach with the Lord.
> Many scenes from my life flashed across the sky.
> In each scene I noticed footprints in the sand.
> Sometimes there were two sets of footprints,
> other times there were one set of footprints.
>
> This bothered me because I noticed
> that during the low periods of my life,
> when I was suffering from
> anguish, sorrow or defeat,
> I could see only one set of footprints.
>
> So I said to the Lord,
> "You promised me Lord,
> that if I followed you,
> you would walk with me always.
> But I have noticed that during
> the most trying periods of my life
> there have only been one
> set of footprints in the sand.
> Why, when I needed you most,
> you have not been there for me?"
>
> The Lord replied,

Chapter 1: Incarnational Spirituality

> "The times when you have
> seen only one set of footprints,
> is when I carried you."

It is obvious that the difficulties, dryness, or distance that we experience in our relationship with God through prayer is not new. The disciples experienced a sleeping Jesus even when he was physically present with them (Mt. 8:24-25; Mk. 4:38-40), and they woke him up. Our daily struggles, and our imagined absence of God were very common among the saints, such as St. John of the Cross, St. Teresa of Avila, St. Catherine of Siena, St. Therese of Lisieux, etc. Thus, there is nothing unusual about experiencing dryness or difficulty in prayer or in our relationship with God. So, when you experience a sleeping God in your life, WAKE HIM UP!

Our fallen nature impacts us so much that we crave relief and consolation rather than struggle. This is also very apparent in our relationships with one another. We thrill in the glory and excitement of friendship but decamp in the face of hardship with the same friend. We find it hard to persevere in a relationship that lacks daily pleasure. Life is not a bed of roses, says a popular maxim. Our world has lured us into this pleasure-seeking attitude that has taken away our ability for longsuffering and endurance. But the Incarnate God, who became one of us, points us to the cross where his love was shone.

To embrace incarnational spirituality is to embrace not only the consolation of the Word made Flesh, but also the way of the cross. "If you want to be my disciple, take up your cross daily and follow me" (Luke 9:23). It is to embrace the joy of Christmas as well as the pain of Good Friday in order to emerge victorious on Easter Sunday with new life! This is the bitter truth! It is our spiritual and human experiences! We will experience inner peace and joy, even with a heavy cross, when we become more humane and gentler in carrying the cross, as well as more compassionate with each other in our dehumanized world! That is incarnational spirituality in action!

REFERENCES:

Motivational Stories. Accessed from http://assets.ngin.com/attachments/document/0040/1426/Motivational_Stories.pdf.

Rolheiser, R. (1999). *The Holy Longing: The Search for a Christian Spirituality.* New York: Doubleday.

Chapter 2

Praying the Angelus with a Humanized God in a Dehumanized World

Sr. Adaku H. Ogbuji, CCVI

The mystery of the Word made flesh, or the humanized God, was captured well by poet Denise Levertov: "God (out of compassion for our ugly failure to evolve) entrusts, as guest, as brother, the Word" (Lacey P. A. & Dewey A, Eds. 2013, *The Collected Poems of Denise Levertov*, p. 1063). Out of love, Jesus became human to redeem our dehumanized and broken world: For God so loved us, that He gave his only begotten Son to make us more human (Jn. 3:16). Our world is dehumanized and ugly because of injustice, racism, lack of tenderness, and compassion toward one another and toward God's creation. Are human beings incarnating enough especially during this pandemic, which scientists think is becoming endemic, and high economic inflation? We are still battling with the outbreak of the Coronavirus pandemic which has the whole world scared and disillusioned. Since the beginning of 2020, the entire world has faced this deadly pandemic with its many variants such as Alpha, Beta, Gamma, Delta, Omicron, etc. Sometimes, new variants emerge and disappear. Other times, new variants persist, like the Delta and Omicron. Is our incarnational process, whatever it might be, as sufficient as it could be or needs to be?

The experience of this global pandemic feels like walking in a lonely desert while feeling the absence of God. At the onset, we experienced loneliness and desired the Jesus who walked on our soil two thousand years ago, in flesh and blood. We desired Jesus with skin as told by Sr. M. Stephanie O'Brien, in her book *Walking With our Ancestors: Ignatian Exercises with the Mother of Jesus and Mary Ward Spirituality*. She told the story of a child who was afraid to sleep alone in a dark room on a stormy night. She calls out to her mom and begs to sleep with her, but she tells her that Jesus is right beside her. The child replies, "But mom, right now I need Jesus with skin on!"

Each of us needed Jesus "with skin on" at the start of the COVID-19 pandemic. Although life is becoming normal this year (2022) since people started getting the vaccines/booster shots. Before then, we experienced an avalanche of fear for so many months, and the clouds were gloomy and bleak. The roads and streets were empty. The Churches were closed for what seemed like an eternity. The number of deaths increased daily. The entire world was at a standstill and imagined the "silence of God" (Ogbuji, 2021). The world was filled with hopelessness, just as when the disciples were hoping that Jesus was the promised Messiah. This longing was captured well by the story of the two disciples on their way to Emmaus (Lk. 24:12-32). "We had hoped…"

The Angelus prayer is a reminder of this hope! In a prayerful way, we recall the moment that the long-awaited hope came to light. The angel Gabriel paid a visit to a young girl—Mary. The angel told her: "Greetings, favored one! The Lord is with you…" Do not be afraid, Mary, for you have found favor with God. You

Chapter 2: Praying the Angelus with a Humanized God

will conceive in your womb and bear a son, and you will name him Jesus. He will be great and will be called the Son of the Most High, and the Lord God will give to him the throne of his ancestor David. He will reign over the house of Jacob forever, and of his kingdom there will be no end" (Lk. 1:26-38).

It is also this hope that we celebrate every year on March 25th—the Solemnity of the Annunciation. It is a feast of hope, when our fear disperses, our hope ignites, and our joy boundless! Isaiah prophesied on this hope: "The people who walked in darkness have seen a great light; those who lived in a land of deep darkness— on them light has shined" (Is. 9:2). The Solemnity of the Annunciation is an important celebration, when the Church commemorates what happened in the history of humanity when the Incarnate Word became flesh after the resounding "YES" of our Blessed Mother Mary. Jesus became one of us, to break the distance between us and God. He is Emmanuel, "God with Us." He became flesh to humanize our world! He became human so that we may become divine.

It is this mystery of the Incarnation of Jesus and his self-emptying (Phil.2:6-8) that we recall when we pray "The Angelus." The Angelus is a Scriptural meditation that points us to Salvation History and the Incarnation story. We meditate on the words of Mary to the angel Gabriel when she gave herself the title: "the Handmaid of the Lord." We join Mary in praying to do God's will, and we invite the Lord "to take flesh" in our lives.

For us, the Congregation of the Sisters of Charity of the Incarnate Word, Houston, the Angelus prayer is especially important. Apart from our individual time to say the Angelus, it is also part of our morning and evening prayer when we pray the breviary as a community and as individuals. In praying the Angelus, we pause to celebrate the mystery of the Incarnation and how we are incarnating the Word by being the healing presence of Jesus. Our incarnational spirituality calls us to enter into a deeper relationship with God who became one of us and whose life mirrors how to be in a relationship with each Sister and those to whom we minister.

The History of the Angelus

The origin of praying the Angelus is dated around the 11th century when Franciscan monks prayed three Hail Marys' along with the bell that was rung at their evening prayer (Fournée, 2000). In 1269, St. Bonaventure proposed that his Franciscan Friars recite these three Hail Marys in the evening after Compline, meditating on the mystery of Christ's Incarnation, while urging at the same time that the recitation always be preceded by the ringing of a bell, so that the brothers and all the faithful nearby would know that it was time for the Hail Mary.

In 1456, Pope Calistus III directed the ringing of the Church's bells every day at noon, and he encouraged Catholics to pray three Hail Marys. The Pope exhorted the faithful to use the noonday prayers to pray for peace in the context of the 15th-century invasion of Europe by the Turks. Thus, the bell rang at noon and became known as the "Peace" bell. At some point in history, an indulgence was granted to those who prayed the Angelus in the morning, at noon, and in the evening. The morning Ave Maria, as it was called, focused on Christ's resurrection, the noontime

Chapter 2: Praying the Angelus with a Humanized God

prayer focused on his Passion, while the evening prayer was for His Incarnation (Fournée, 2000).

Toward the end of the 16th century, the Angelus became the prayer as we know it today with three Hail Marys and short verses in between (called versicles), ending with a concluding prayer. It was first published in modern form in a catechism around 1560 in Venice. At this time, the Angelus was said kneeling, but Pope Benedict XIV directed that the Angelus be recited while standing, and he exhorted that, during the Easter Season, the Regina Caeli (Queen of Heaven Rejoice) be said instead of the Angelus.

The Angelus reminds us of the angel Gabriel's visit to Mary announcing God's plan for her. It retells Mary's faith and her desire to collaborate with God's plan. It unveils the mystery of the Incarnation and our Lord's Passion and Resurrection. It is a prayer that invites us to meditate on God's greatest love for humanity. Praying the Angelus at noon interrupts our daily routine, so that we turn our thoughts to God, to our Blessed Mother, and to the mystery of the Word made Flesh who taught us to pray without ceasing (Lk 18:1; 1Thess. 5:17).

In meditating on and living incarnational spirituality, we discover the sacredness in each person; we discover the need to practice compassion and see Christ in all people, as well as the need to stand as agents of transformation and social justice. It inspires us to live in harmony with others who are different from us, rather than building walls between "us and them." The Incarnate Word mirrored how to live in a dehumanized world. He spent time with sinners and ate with them. He touched the untouchables in society and let himself be touched. He reached out to the poor and the discriminated. The Spirituality of the Incarnation, embedded in the Angelus prayer, challenges us to commit to eliminating the walls that bring discrimination, violence, prejudice, bigotry, or racism, and to build bridges in a world of walls and dehumanization.

In our broken and dehumanized world, we witnessed the "Black Lives Matter" marches in many cities of the United States in 2020, because of the killing of George Floyd. We have witnessed hate crimes against Asians. We have witnessed in the U.S. how the caste system uses skin colour to assign privileges, especially favouring the "white skin." This white supremacy is also found in religious communities which calls us to be attentive to our biases. "Ignorance is not an excuse," says Sr. Elise D. Garcia. How we treat one another matters!

Sr. Elise D. García, OP, explained it well in her Presidential address during the LCWR (Leadership Conference of Women Religious) general assembly in August 2021: "The Black people have remained at the bottom of the caste system. Regardless of their education, career achievements, material wealth or other markers of status, our Black sisters and brothers, to this day, live under the oppression of a menacing caste system that daily abases." Quoting historian Claudia Koonz, Sr. Elise pointed out how the Nazi government was perplexed that the "American people, in the land of the free, seemed to accept their racial hierarchy "as natural." Hitler also "praised the United States' near genocide of Native Americans and the exiling to reservations of those who had survived." Isabel Wilkerson (2020), in her famous book *Caste: The Origins of Our Discontents,* also expressed how "the Nazis were impressed by the

American custom of lynching its subordinate caste of African Americans." According to Wilkerson, "Hitler was pleased that the US had shot down the millions of redskins to a few hundred thousand. He marvelled at their ability to maintain an air of robust innocence in the wake of mass death and wondered why the United States was condemning his racial purification" (p. 81). We are not different from Hitler if we use skin colour to segregate or exclude people whom we are called to love and accept. Garcia encouraged religious communities to be attentive to the way we exclude some members because of their skin colour or level of education. According to her, "The way of the cross is giving over of oneself to the radical love and solidarity that Jesus lived; extending ourselves as kin to all who are marginalized, excluded, and disinherited. It is standing at the foot of the cross where unbearable suffering is lifted by grace" (Garcia, 2021).

Our world is also crippled by selfishness, greed, envy, poverty, hunger, wars, terrorist attack, insecurity, manmade and natural disasters, etc. We are neither compassionate to the created universe nor to ourselves. Just imagine what could happen or how our world would look like if everyone was to practice a little kindness! There would be genuine love, peace, forgiveness, kindness, joy, happiness, selfless service, and the world's wealth would be enough for everyone. This reminded me of the classic and popular song *"Try a Little Kindness,"* written by Curt Sapaugh and Bobby Austin, and first recorded by American country music singer Glen Campbell:

> If you see your brother standing by the road
> With a heavy load from the seeds he sowed
> And if you see your sister falling by the way
> Just stop and say, "You're going the wrong way."
> You've got to try a little kindness
> Yes, show a little kindness
> Just shine your light for everyone to see
> And if you try a little kindness
> Then you'll overlook the blindness
> Of narrow-minded people on the narrow-minded streets.

When we try a little kindness, we overlook the blindness of the narrow-minded people. When we look at the opposite side rather than trying a little kindness in our world smitten by a global pandemic, then we are a "narrow-minded people on the narrow-minded streets!" Similarly, we are no different from the Levite and the priest in the story of the Good Samaritan (Lk 10:25-37). The priest and the Levite, though they were observing the Jewish ritual law, were like narrow-minded people on a narrow-minded street who could not try a little kindness. They placed observance of law above the work of charity. Of course, they were right, but never kind! And as I think of them, I recall the refrain of a song by Hubert Dapliyan: "Better to be kind than be right, A gentle heart conquers a blazing fire. Better to be kind than be right, A humble spirit conquers a mile of pride."

Chapter 2: Praying the Angelus with a Humanized God

But a foreigner, an outsider, a Samaritan, whom the wounded Jewish man would have never associated with under normal circumstances, was the one who bent over in love and tried a little kindness. He offered his money, his oil, his donkey, and his time to save a life. Mother Theresa of Calcutta expressed it this way: "No one can love unless it is at their own expense." At his own expense, the Good Samaritan became the only hope and a lit candle that pushed away the darkness that surrounded the bruised man. Each of us can be a lit candle in the darkened lives of others. Our flicker of light can shatter the shield of darkness brought about by our cold and wounded world. This light begins with "you" who is reading this book, and also with me who wrote this reflection. Jesus asked us to "Go and do likewise; go and humanize our broken world; go and show a little kindness with much love; go and listen to the cry of the poor; go and love."

It was Pope Francis who said: "I prefer a church which is bruised, hurting and dirty because it has been out on the streets, rather than a church which is unhealthy from being confined and from clinging to its own security" (*Evangelii Gaudium*, no 49). The pandemic is a global one! We are all suffering! The world is hurting because of economic hardship, inflation, and the war in Ukraine! We need to do our piece by showing a little kindness and work toward promoting the common good. We need to lay down our weapons of war and embrace peace, justice, and reconciliation, in order to become more divine and humanized.

Pope Francis in *Evangelii Gaudium* (no 9-10, 49) also explains: "If we wish to lead a dignified and fulfilling life, we have to reach out to others and seek their good. Life grows by being given away, and it weakens in isolation and comfort. Indeed, those who enjoy life most are those who leave security on the shore and become excited by the mission of communicating life to others…. while at our door people are starving and Jesus does not tire of saying to us: 'Give them something to eat'" (Mk 6:37).

In following the Word made Flesh and in living the spirituality of incarnation, we are to obey his will and follow in his footsteps. This is because incarnational spirituality is the spirituality of compassion, love, and tenderness toward all of God's creation. The tenderness that enables us to listen to the silent cry of the polluted earth and the poor among us. This tenderness comes from within and has the power to heal and bring us closer to God. In living this spirituality, we strive to become more human as the Incarnate Word. And by grace, we become what He is by nature—Divine. Subsequently, our praying and meditating on the Angelus become even more authentic, real, and incarnational.

REFERENCES

Lacey P. A. & Dewey A, Eds. (2013). The Collected Poems of Denise Levertov. New York: New Directions.

Fournée, J. (2000). *Praying the Angelus.* New York: Crossroad Publishing Company.

Garcia, E. D. (2021). Presidential Address: Creating Space for the Future: Cutting Deeper Grooves of Transforming Love into Evolution. 2021 Virtual Assembly of the Leadership Conference of Women Religious (LCWR) August 11-13th.

Motivational Stories. Accessed from http://assets.ngin.com/attachments/document/0040/1426/Motivational_Stories.pdf.

O'Brien, S. (2002). *Walking With our Ancestors: Ignatian Exercises with the Mother of Jesus and Mary Ward Spirituality.* Nairobi, Kenya: Paulines Publications Africa.

Ogbuji, A. H. (2021). *Out of the Lips of Infants, Wisdom Comes: Retelling the Bible Stories.* Nairobi, Kenya: Franciscan Kolbe Press.

Pope Francis. (2013). *Evangelii Gaudium* (The Joy of the Gospel). Accessed from https://www.vatican.va/content/francesco/en/apost_exhortations/documents/papa-francesco_esortazione-ap_20131124_evangelii-gaudium.html.

Wilkerson, I. (2020). *Caste: The Origins of our Discontents.* New York: Random House.

Chapter 3

Incarnational Spirituality: The Spirituality of Compassion

Sr. Adaku H. Ogbuji, CCVI

"A little bit of compassion makes the world less cold and more just." —Pope Francis (*Evangelii Gaudium*, no. 49. Compassion is derived from two Latin words: "com," which means "together with" and "pati" which means "to suffer." Literally, it means "to suffer together with" or "to feel together with." Compassion is the empathetic consciousness of others' distress and the desire to alleviate it. It has the combination of love, concern, consideration, empathy, care, forgiveness, and kindness (Ogbuji, 2021). Compassion is fueled by love; and as such, everybody needs it. Its significance can be felt in different spheres of life, such as in healthcare systems, shopping malls, banking halls, government parastatals, commercial centers, business companies, schools of different levels, religious communities, families, online platforms, sports fields, legal companies, humanitarian and social works, entertainment companies and artists, Churches, and the entire world. The obvious thing is that every human being is capable of demonstrating compassion, and we don't have to be in a relationship with the person who is receiving our compassion.

Sometimes, we confuse love with compassion: Love is a commandment and a thing of the heart. But one can choose to show compassion to a homeless person on the road begging for alms or a stranger in need of assistance without any prior relationship.

    A woman went to McDonald's to buy a hamburger for lunch in the United States. It was during the winter, and no one was allowed to sit inside the restaurant unless they had ordered a meal or a drink. Inside this fast-food place were three street boys who were looking for a warm place to stay for a while. They ordered what they could afford—three cups of coffee. Probably sipping their coffee in anticipation of some kind-hearted person noticing their plight and realizing that they were hungry. They wouldn't beg because there was a sign outside saying: "No soliciting." Unfortunately, due to the unpleasant odor of the poor boys, some of the customers inside began leaving. However, one woman inside noticed what was happening. After enjoying her meal, she ordered another three hamburger meals, which she took over and handed to the boys. Filled with joy, they thanked the woman and felt so grateful because drinking coffee on an empty stomach is not fun.

Compassion is shown to everyone, even to a stranger, by looking into each person's eyes and listening attentively without judgment. It was James R. Fisher, Jr., who said: "The greatest virtue is kindness. You can't love everyone, but you can be kind to everyone." Compassion is shown by taking time with each person, by treating rudeness or disrespect with kindness, by being patient with those who seem slow to understand, by sharing our gifts, by being gentle with ourselves and others, by loving especially those who are the hardest to love, and by forgiving those who hurt us. Through this virtue we learn how to listen to our brothers/sisters empathically, accept them, and have hearts that will move us to act in a humane way. The book of Tobit captures it well when it says: "Do to no one what you yourself dislike. Give to the hungry some of your bread, and to the naked some of your clothing. Whatever you have left over, give away as alms; and do not resent the alms you give" (Tb. 4:14b-16). Compassion exists without a relationship. It is selfless! It does not demand anything in return, and it is unconditional.

    Mark was walking home from school one day when he noticed a fellow student ahead of him had tripped and dropped all of the books he was carrying, along with two sweaters, a baseball bat, a glove and a small tape recorder. Mark knelt down and helped the boy pick up the scattered articles. Since they were going the same way, he helped to carry part of the burden. As they walked and told stories, Mark discovered the boy's name was Bill, that he loved video games, baseball and history, that he was having lots of trouble with some subjects at school, and that he had just broken up with his girlfriend.

    The two arrived at Bill's home first and Mark was invited in for a cold drink and to watch some television. The afternoon passed pleasantly with a few laughs and some shared small talk, then Mark went home. They continued to see each other around school, had lunch together once or twice, then both graduated from junior high school. They ended up in the same high school where they had brief contacts over the years. Finally, the long-awaited senior year came and three weeks before graduation, Bill asked Mark if they could talk.

Bill reminded him of the day, many years ago, when they met for the first time. "Did you ever wonder why I was carrying so many things home that day?" asked Bill. Bill continued; "You see, I cleaned out my school locker because I didn't want to leave a mess for anyone else. I had stored away some of my mother's sleeping pills and I was going home to commit suicide. But after we spent some time together talking and laughing, I realized that if I had killed myself, I would have missed that time and so many others that would follow. So, you see, Mark, when you picked up those books that day, you did a lot more. You saved my life." -John W. Schlatter (Accessed from the Motivational Stories).

Compassion is an empathic feeling. It involves the willingness to put yourself in someone else's shoes, to take the focus off yourself and to imagine what it's like to be in someone else's predicament, and simultaneously, to feel love for that person. The letter of St. Peter describes this scenario well when it says: "You should all have unity of spirit and be sympathetic, love one another, have compassion and a humble mind…It is for this that you were called—that you might inherit a blessing" (1 Peter 3:8-9). This is what Mark did without knowing that he was saving a life, Bill's life.

I wonder how the story would have ended if Mark hadn't stopped to help a stranger he had met on his way home from school. I am sure you know the answer! Compassion cannot exist in isolation of self. We have to be compassionate with ourselves before we can give it to others.

Self-Compassion

Self-compassion is the attitude of treating oneself kindly and non-judgmentally. Lack of it is seen when we scold ourselves or hold anger against ourselves or others for long hours, days, weeks, or even months after some sort of failure. Sometimes, we dwell in self-pity, unforgiveness, and allow a negative attitude to ruin our lives, thereby hurting ourselves. Let us ask ourselves: Are we compassionate toward ourselves? If your compassion does not include yourself, it is incomplete. When we embrace self-compassion, we are then in a better position to extend this virtue to others.

Michael is the kind of guy you would love to befriend. He is always in a good mood and always has something positive to say. When someone would ask him how he was doing, he would reply, "If I were any better, I would be twins!" He was a natural motivator. If an employee was having a bad day, Michael was there telling the employee how to look on the positive side of the situation. Seeing this style really made me curious, so one day I went up to Michael and asked him, "I don't get it! You can't be a positive person all the time. How do you do it?" Michael replied,

"Each morning I wake up and say to myself, 'Mike, you have two choices today: You can choose to be compassionate to yourself or you can choose to be hard on yourself.' I choose to be compassionate to myself. Each time something bad happens, I can choose to be a victim or I can choose to learn from it. I choose to learn from it. Every time someone comes to me complaining, I can choose to accept their complaint or I can point out the positive side of life. I choose the positive side of life." "Yeah, right, it isn't that easy," I protested. "Yes, it is," Michael said. "Life is all about choices. When you cut away all the junk and baggage that prevent self-compassion, then life becomes simpler. In every situation we make choices. You choose how you react to situations. You choose how people will affect your mood. You choose to be in a good mood or a bad mood. The bottom line is: It's your choice how you live your life." Author Unknown (from forwarded WhatsApp Message).

The choices we make in life can make us or break us. Sometimes we take Advil, Paracetamol, or some kind of pain relief pill for another person's headache. This is not saying that we should not help people, but it is not okay to choose a negative attitude for whatever life may bring us. I am the one who chooses how I will live my day when I wake up in the morning. If I practice self-compassion, then I will spend the day in an optimistic attitude rather than in grumbling. I found the wise saying below very important for daily decisions:

I woke up early today, excited over all I get to do before the clock strikes midnight. Because I am important, my job is to choose what kind of day I am going to have. Today I can complain because the weather is rainy, or I can be thankful that the grass is getting watered for free. Today I can feel sad that I don't have more money, or I can be glad that my finances encourage me to plan my purchases wisely and guide me away from waste. Today I can grumble about my health, or I can rejoice that I am alive. Today I can lament over all that my parents didn't give me when I was growing up, or I can feel grateful that they allowed me to be born. Today I can cry because roses have thorns, or I can celebrate their beautiful roses. Today I can mourn my lack of friends, or I can excitedly embark upon a quest to discover new relationships. Today I can whine because I have to go to work, or I can shout for joy because I have a job to do. Today I can complain because I have to go to school, or I can eagerly open my mind and fill it with rich new knowledge. Today I can murmur dejectedly because I have to do housework, or I can feel honored because the Lord has provided shelter for my mind, body and soul. Today stretches ahead of me, waiting to be shaped. And here I am, the sculptor who gets to do the shaping. What today will be like is up to me. I get to choose what kind of day I will have! (Author unknown, Accessed from the Motivational Stories).

Self-compassion is associated with a positive attitude and a grateful heart. Having self-compassion reduces burn-out, depression, and anxiety. It increases well-being, positive aging, and happiness in life. It is said that "it is not the happy people who are grateful. It is the grateful people who are happy." I can turn it around and say: "It is not the happy people who are compassionate. It is the compassionate people who are happy.

Being kind to self is a way of recognizing one's inability to be perfect and to see oneself from a comforting rather than critical perspective. Becoming aware of when we are reacting or in any way judging ourselves is the first step. The second step is to become present with how our bodies, minds, and hearts respond to the experience of pain. Setting an intentional goal to be kind toward ourselves is what helps us to connect with compassion.

The importance of compassion cannot be over-emphasized. Research has confirmed that showing compassion, empathy, and kindness to people leads to healing. Patients have reported that clinician's empathy and compassion is related to increased patient satisfaction and lower distress (Lelorain, Brédart, Dolbeault, & Sultan, 2012). Brief expressions of compassion expressed by doctors are related to a decrease in patient's anxiety (Fogarty, et al., 1999), associated with higher patient survival rates (Ironson et al., 2017), and promotes social connection among adults and children (Seppala et al., 2013).

While medication holds the power to cure, care delivered with kindness and compassion can speed up the healing process and lead to better outcomes for patients and caregivers alike. Showing compassion, offering reassurance, and listening attentively calm a wounded person, reduce pain, lower blood pressure, and enable faster recuperation. It also leads to emotional healing and world peace. Compassion-focused therapy is reported as a promising therapeutic approach for individuals with affective disorders characterized by high self-criticism (Leaviss & Uttley, 2012).

Compassion promotes positive parenting by improving parent-child relationships, with more affection and less negative affect (Duncan, Coatsworth, & Greenberg, 2009). Compassion within classrooms is related to increased cooperation and better learning (Hart & Kindle Hodson, 2004). Compassion for teachers as expressed by colleagues is linked to increased teacher job satisfaction, organizational commitment, and sense of emotional vigor (Eldor & Shoshani, 2016). Compassion expressed as a function of service work is related to improved health and well-being among volunteers (Black & Living, 2004; Yum & Lightfoot, 2005). Individuals who have high levels of self-compassion or compassion for others respond to stress in a healthier way than those who are found wanting in this area.

In their research, Neff et al. (2007) discovered that self-compassion is linked to various aspects of general well-being, such as reducing feelings of anxiety, depression, and rumination. Self-compassion also reduces burnout and fosters important adaptive qualities among medical professionals (Mills & Chapman, 2016). Self-compassion is linked to more positive aging (Phillips & Ferguson, 2013).

These research results go a long way in demonstrating that, when we practice self-compassion, we become capable of truly and consciously giving love to our world. It was H.H. the Dalai Lama, a Buddhist Guru, who said: "The whole purpose of religion is to facilitate love, compassion, and forgiveness. If you want others to be happy, practice compassion. If you want to be happy, practice compassion." Compassion does not communicate weakness, rather absolute strength, and each person has the ability to enliven and enrich the world around us by being a source of compassion to others. Of course, we are following the footsteps of our compassionate God through His Son who is an epitome of compassion as depicted in the Scriptures.

Compassion in the Scriptures

The word compassion is mentioned eighty-four times in the Scripture. It is one of the attributes of God (Ex. 34:6-7 and Ps. 86:15): "The LORD the LORD, merciful and compassionate, slow to anger, abounding in steadfast love and faithfulness." We share this attribute with God because we are made in his image and likeness. Compassion makes us god-like and to see with God's eyes, even when some people doubt the existence of a compassionate God in a broken world.

> There is a parable of a king who went hunting with his servant when unexpectedly a wild animal attacked them and the king lost his little finger on one hand. He said to his servant, "You made me believe that God is compassionate and good, but see now, God did not protect me." But the servant replied, "God is compassionate and he is to be trusted." This enraged the king so much, that he had the

servant thrown in prison. Then the next time he went hunting, he was by himself. This time he was captured by some barbarians who practiced human's sacrifice. However, on the sacrificial altar, the savages discovered that their sacrificial item was incomplete because he was missing a finger. He was released because he was considered unfit as a sacrifice to their gods. On his return to the palace, he ordered the release of his servant and said to him: "Now I believe that God is compassionate and good for I was almost killed today, but God saved me. However, why did God allow me to put you into prison if He cares for you?"

"If I had gone with you," replied the servant, "I would have been used as a sacrifice to the gods because I have all my fingers. So, know this O king! The Lord is compassionate and good." (Singapore Christian, accessed March 2022, from https://www.singaporechristian.com).

Sometimes, it is difficult to believe in a compassionate God in a world filled with agonies, pandemics, and so much sufferings, wars, and deaths. But God, out of compassion, did not spare his own Son from dying. He sacrificed His only Son for our sake.

Similarly, Jesus lived out this attribute of compassion just like His Father. Jesus was always moved with compassion before performing many of his miracles, like the feeding narratives (Mk. 8.2; Mt. 14.14), the healing of the widow's only son at Nain (Lk. 7:11-17), or the healing of the blind men (Mt. 20.32-34). Jesus respected, dined with, and listened to those that society normally looked down upon, including women and notorious sinners. He performed his compassionate acts/signs/miracles even on Sabbath days.

In his compassionate heart, Jesus entered the suffering of the people of his time, he preached the good news to them, he healed their sicknesses, he raised their dead, he gave sight to their blind, he fed the hungry, he delivered those possessed by evil spirits, he identified with the poor, and finally he died on the cross. Jesus demonstrated so much compassion in his parables and teachings. e.g., the parable of the Prodigal Son (Lk. 15:11-32); the parable of the Good Samaritan, which clearly shows the power of compassion (Lk. 10:25-37), the parable of the king who had compassion on his servant and forgave his debt, showing how we should forgive one another (Mt. 18:21-35). Jesus made it very clear that he desires compassion/mercy and not sacrifice (Mt. 9:13). Jesus, through compassion, showed us how to be fully human.

Incarnational spirituality is a spirituality of compassion. It's the recognition that other people's pain and frustrations are as real as our own, sometimes far worse. In recognizing this fact and trying to offer some assistance, we open our hearts to become more human: that is, to love more, to be kind and ultimately to forgive just as we have been forgiven; for whatsoever we do to the least of our brothers and sisters, we do to Christ (Mt. 25:40).

We need compassion today in our world in order to make a difference. We should feel for others and be concerned about what is happening in the lives of our community members, friends, family members and co-workers. The road to compassion is not usually filled with roses and rainbows. Actually, compassion is of-

Chapter 3: Incarnational Spirituality: The Spirituality of Compassion

ten learned through having experienced deep pain, betrayal, hurtful feelings, and broken trust. Thus, we use the same help that we have received and extend it to others (2 Cor. 1:4), especially to those with whom we live and work. Our Constitutions tell us: "As bearers of the Gospel of Love, we strive to demonstrate a love without limit for all, especially for the poor and suffering and those with whom we live and work" (Article 3). Sometimes, we love the poor outside, which is great, but we fail to recognize the suffering and poverty of those we live with!

Compassion moves us to become aware of the people who are suffering, wherever they are, and wanting to do something. Even when we have no material things to offer, we can offer our smiles, listening heart, an appropriate touch, words of kindness or a support. These small gestures are capable of transforming into something wonderful and priceless for the receiver.

Compassion is the path of choice for courageous men and women. It is not for the weak, and it is not a weakness! It is fortitude! It is part of being human! In becoming human, Jesus took the path of compassion. He humbled himself and lived his entire life offering compassion and care to those in need. Jesus descended to our level and practiced the real and concrete language of compassion and love.

We are human and are called to be more humane. Pope Francis, in *The Joy of the Gospel* (no. 8) explains: "We become fully human when we become more than human, when we let God bring us beyond ourselves in order to attain the fullest truth of our being...For if we have received the love which restores meaning to our lives, how can we fail to share that love with others?" Jesus' compassion gives meaning to our lives. He was committed to helping us become whole and more humane. He loved us even when we were still sinners (Rm. 5:8). How can we fail to show compassion to others as much as we have received? We are called to continue this mission of Jesus, by helping ourselves and others become fully human through compassion.

REFERENCES:

Motivational Stories. Accessed from http://assets.ngin.com/attachments/document/0040/1426/Motivational_Stories.pdf.

Ogbuji A. H. (2021). *Out of the Lips of Infants, Wisdom Comes: Retelling the Bible Stories.* Nairobi, Kenya: Franciscan Kolbe Press.

Pope Francis: *Evangelii Gaudium* (2013). (The Joy of the Gospel) Accessed from https://www.vatican.va/content/francesco/en/apost_exhortations/documents/papa-francesco_esortazione-ap_20131124_evangelii-gaudium.html.

Singapore Christian. Accessed from https://www.singaporechristian.com

Chapter 4

Incarnational Spirituality and the Care of Creation

Sr. Margret Bulmer, CCVI

Incarnational spirituality is a call to reverence all of Creation, to care for it and to follow the example of Jesus the Incarnate Word in living this commitment. As a Sister of Charity of the Incarnate Word, Houston, our charism is based on the life of Jesus Incarnate in our world. Jesus came and lived among us, He cherished the Earth and all its inhabitants. This is our call, too. When Jesus roamed the hills and valleys of Nazareth as a child, he became imbued with a love of God's creation. He walked on this earth, he breathed our air, and he contemplated about the soil, harvest, seed, etc. When he preached to the people, he used examples of nature, trees, sheep, wild birds, and people to tell his stories. He knew the connections between the people, the animals, the fields, the flowers, and all living and growing things. Like Jesus, we all have stories to tell of our connections to nature.

Through the mystery of the Incarnation, Jesus became one with nature and inserted himself, not only into historic reality but also into cosmic reality. Pope Francis, in his encyclical, *Laudato Si'*, revealed a new relationship with nature and a sense of responsibility and commitment to God's creatures. Our Spirituality, therefore, calls us to be ecologically compassionate and just in our lifestyles and behaviors.

When I was in ministry as a nurse in one of our hospitals, I was working the 3-11 shift. It was close to midnight when I finally made my way home to the convent which was just across the street. One time, I paused for a minute to look up at the sky and was mesmerized by the number of stars I could see. I stood in the middle of the street and felt such a strong connection to the stars. I just wanted to stay there forever. Since then, stars have fascinated me, and at night I always go looking for them. We are all so connected to each other, and no one is an island.

Another experience that fascinates me has to do with the Sycamore tree outside my window. It is beautifully shaped and a great example of displaying all four seasons, which in turn reflect the cycles of life. We are born, we grow and develop, we mature and then we decline. Everything is so connected, and if we pay attention to the seasons, to nature and to ourselves as we go through life, we see the beautiful plan of God in the Universe. As Christians we must realize the value of our position by not taking Incarnation and Creation seriously. We should not fail to revere the Earth as God's gift to us, something to be cherished and cared for. The whole world is one body, and all the parts must work together, so that fitting honor and praise may be given to the creator, God.

So, what are Christians called to do? We must realize that we are not at the center of the universe, and that all else is here for our good. The term "Eco Conversion" is the realization that humanity is part of the community of the Earth. Eco Conversion is turning away from human self-centeredness, and toward understanding ourselves as part of the network of life, truly seeing that everything is interrelated. If we follow these rules of the Earth, change will

Chapter 4: Incarnational Spirituality and the Care of Creation

happen. The rules are: 1) Take only your share. 2) Clean up after yourself. 3) Keep the Earth in good repair for those who will use it later. (Sallie McFague)

What do the Scientists say about Climate Change and the Earth?

For many years, professional scientists from around the world have been trying to wake us up to what we are doing to Mother Earth. Trying to help us realize how our actions and ways of living are damaging the ecosystems, causing millions of animals to become extinct, warming the oceans and in turn destroying coral reefs and causing waters to rise and swallow up islands where people live. The science of climate change is firmly settled, and we don't need more facts to tell us so. I quote from "Under the Sky We Make" by Kimberly Nicholas, PhD: "The Science of Climate Change is firmly settled and has been for a very long time. It boils down to just five key facts: It's warming. It's us. We're sure. It's bad. But, we can fix it." Humans have the capacity to stop dangerously destabilizing the climate. Yes, we can, if we listen with our hearts to the cry of the earth (Romans 8:22-23) that is groaning. The present suffering of creation is very real, and we are called to fix it!

Major Religious Groups work together to combat climate change

Since incarnational spirituality encompasses the whole world, it is only natural that religious groups throughout the world would work together on climate issues. We are fortunate today to have so many leaders of various religions to encourage us to take up our responsibility and do our part to save our planet. We are blessed to have Pope Francis leading the Church at this time. With his understanding and compassionate heart, he is well aware of the beauty of creation, of Jesus' incarnation into that creation, and our call to live that incarnation in our own lives.

> "The Father is the ultimate source of everything, the loving and self-communicating foundation of all that exists. The Son, his reflection, through whom all things were created, united himself to this earth when he was formed in the womb of Mary. The Spirit, infinite bond of love, is ultimately present at the very heart of the universe, inspiring and bringing new pathways. Consequently, when we contemplate with wonder the universe in all its grandeur and beauty, we must praise the whole Trinity." (*Laudato Si*, p. 137)

If God has given us the Universe, and Jesus is the Incarnational Embodiment of that gift, what then is our response to the invitation to be signs of the Incarnation in our world?

We are called to convert ourselves to Integral Ecology. What does this mean? If we want to practice and live by incarnational spirituality, we must understand the ecology of the Earth and the relationship between living organisms and the environment in which they develop. We must experience Ecological Conversion in our own lives, and then encourage it in the lives of others. This

Chapter 4: Incarnational Spirituality and the Care of Creation

conversion calls for a number of attitudes which together foster a spirit of generous care, full of tenderness.

The greatest among them is the attitude of gratitude. This is a recognition that the world is God's loving gift, and that we are called quietly to imitate his generosity through self-sacrifice and good works, to have a loving awareness that we are not disconnected from the rest of the creatures but joined in a splendid universal communion. As believers, we do not look at the world from without, but from within, conscious of the bonds with which God has linked us to all beings.

Another religious leader is Rev. Robert E. Shore-Goss of the United Church of Christ in North Hollywood, California. His book *God is Green: an Eco-Spirituality of Incarnate Compassion* follows the incarnational spirituality of Jesus. His congregation has made "the Earth" a member of their parish. He fosters ecological conversation in the Church and outlines the following practices for congregations: meditating on nature, inviting sermons on green topics, covenanting with the Earth, and retrieving the natural elements of the Sacraments. He says: "If we fall in love with God's Creation, then we will fight to save the earth!"

The Buddhist Declaration on Climate Change, published in October 2015, welcomed climate-change statements from other religious traditions. It called for the phasing out of fossil fuels, and challenged world leaders to generate the political will to close the emissions gap left by country climate pledges, in order to ensure that the global temperature increase remains below 1.5 degrees.

The Hindu Declaration of November 2015 reached into Hinduism's own unique experiences of nature and called for greater harmony among all living beings. The Declaration quoted the Mahabharata, which states that "dharma exists for the welfare of all beings." Life must be treated with respect. It asks the world's 900 million Hindus to make the transition to clean energy, adopt a plant-based diet, and lead lives in harmony with the natural world.

The Islamic Climate Change Declaration affirms the intimacy of God with creation. The declaration sees the divinely ordered cosmology of creation as imperiled by human disregard of its designated role in the wider context of things. We face the distinct possibility that our species could be responsible for ending life as we know it on our planet. This current rate of climate change cannot be sustained, and the earth's fine balance (mizan) may soon be lost.

The Jewish Environmental and Energy Imperative, signed by 50 Jewish leaders across the religious and political spectrum, established a goal of reducing Jewish community greenhouse gases by 84% by the year 2050. It encouraged a community-wide approach to greening synagogues, homes, and buildings. Many Jews tend to be on the liberal to progressive side of the political spectrum, they have long been active on social issues. Therefore, the area of environment and climate change, in particular, is no exception.

It is clear from his Encyclical *Laudato Si* that Pope Francis wants Catholics to work with these great faiths on issues such as climate change. Cooperation among religions on crucial issues such as climate change is so important in our modern world.

Chapter 4: Incarnational Spirituality and the Care of Creation

In light of all of this, what can I do to combat climate change? Some advice from Pope Francis in *Laudato Si* includes:

- Work toward a new lifestyle

Developed countries are in a whirlwind of needless buying and selling which we call extreme consumerism. We have come to believe that this is reasonable and leads us to believe that we are free as long as we have the supposed freedom to consume. Obsession with a consumerist lifestyle can only lead to violence and destruction. But all is not lost. Today, the issue of environmental degradation challenges us to examine our own lifestyle. We must become aware and awaken to a new reverence for life, and a firm resolve to attain sustainability. Let's join in the struggle for justice and peace and the joyful celebration of life.

- Educate ourselves about the environment

An awareness of the gravity of today's cultural and ecological crisis must be translated into new habits. Environmental education has broadened its goals. It also seeks to restore various levels of ecological equilibrium, by establishing harmony within ourselves, with others, with nature, with other living creatures and with God. Be aware of educational opportunities available in your community and collaborate with others in this endeavor. Education must not only supply information, but also provide motivation toward the goal of instilling new habits.

- Work toward Ecological Conversion

Ecological conversion is first and foremost realizing that we have personally harmed the Earth. We must repent of our disregard for the Earth and experience a real conversion and change of heart. But this change of heart cannot be only on an individual level. It must be a community experience of ecological conversion, and then change will begin to happen.

- Prophetic and contemplative lifestyle

If we personally take on the prophetic role of showing the way to ecological conversion and a change of heart, then our lifestyle will reflect the changes we want to make. Contemplation of the gifts of God's Creation will encourage us and make us realize that we need one another to accomplish this great mission.

In conclusion, I offer A Prayer for the Earth:

All powerful God, you are present in the whole universe
And in the smallest of creatures.
You embrace with your tenderness all that exists.
Pour out upon us the power of your love so that we may protect life and beauty.
Fill us with your peace, that we may live as brothers and sisters harming no one. Amen.

References:

Pope Francis. (2015). *Laudato Si: On Care for Our Common Home*

Nicholas, K. (2021). *Under the Sky we Make: How to Be Human in a Warming World.* New York: G.P. Putnam's Sons

Shore-Goss, R.E. (2016). *God is Green: An Eco Spirituality of Incarnate Compassion.* Eugene, OR: Cascade Books.

Rohr, Richard. (2018). *Creation Is the Body of God.* Accessed https://cac.org/creation-is-the-body-of-god-2018-02-19/

Chapter 5

Incarnational Spirituality and Forgiveness

Sr. Adaku H. Ogbuji, CCVI

Just imagine a world without forgiveness! Life would surely be unbearable! It would be like a world without life or love. A world that is cold and heartless! In his opening address to the Second Vatican Council participants, Pope John XXIII said: "The Church must make use of the medicine of mercy rather than that of severity. She must show herself to be a loving mother of all, benign, patient, full of mercy and goodness" (McBrien, R, 2012). Without forgiveness and mercy toward ourselves and others, we would be chained to the suffering of the past. When someone betrays you, you can hate them, or at some point you can say: "It's not worth it." It is not life-giving to live day after day with hatred in your heart. The person who might have wronged you could be living a good life somewhere else, probably not even aware of how much you are hurting. Who is suffering then? Yet, there you are trapped in your tiny little world, hating them and suffering as a result of bottled anger, rage, unforgiveness, malice, and fury.

Forgiveness is a virtue and the only real path to freedom when it comes to healing hurt. Sometimes, we don't realize how much we hurt ourselves and others by unforgiveness. Forgiveness is the process of a conscious and deliberate decision to release feelings of resentment or vengeance toward a person or group who has harmed us, regardless of whether they actually deserve our forgiveness.

Forgiveness does not deny or diminish the seriousness of an offense against us. It does not mean forgetting, nor does it mean condoning or excusing offenses; rather, it brings the forgiver a peace of mind and frees them from corrosive anger and resentment, by letting go of deeply held negative feelings. When we harbour grudges and so much hatred for long a time, it can eat us up from the inside out. Our Pastor, Monsignor Henry Breier, at the Cathedral Basilica of St. Louis, Missouri, USA, puts it well: "By unforgiveness, we drink rat poison, and wait for the rat to die." However, through the process of forgiveness, we empower ourselves to recognize the pain we are suffering, without letting that pain define us, enabling us to heal and move on with life.

The story of St. Josephine Bakhita comes to my mind as I think of the genuine and healing power of forgiveness and incarnational spirituality. She was a Sudanese woman who was sold into slavery when she was between seven and nine years old (1877). Between 1877 and 1889, she was sold and resold into slavery, and she suffered oppression by the majority of her slave owners. There were 114 marks on her body as proof of the torture she endured. She later joined the Cannossian Sisters in 1893 after severe and brutal treatment by her slave masters. Once a student asked her: "What would you do, if you were to meet your captors?" Without hesitation, she responded: "If I were to meet those who kidnapped me, and even those who tortured me, I would kneel and kiss their hands. For, if these things had not happened, I would not have been a Christian and a religious sister today." Throughout her life she kept a cheerful disposition, and people were drawn to her because of her gentleness and calm spirit. She was called "Black Mother" (Madre Moretta) (John Paul Meenan, 2022, "The Hope and Forgiveness of Josephine Bakhita," *Catholic Insight*).

I am sure the student was expecting a different answer, maybe one that sounded more like revenge, or perhaps even an asking of God to fight for her. But St. Bakhita chose the power of embodying the power of healing. Jesus tells us "Make friends with your opponents" (Mt. 5:25). Abraham Lincoln echoes the same "You destroy an enemy by making him a friend." Mahatma Gandhi also held the same opinion: "When you are confronted by an enemy, conquer him with love."

Just imagine returning kind words and forgiving gestures to the person who abuses or hates you. You have surely disarmed them! This is done by: offering them help if they are clearly in some need, focusing on their good qualities, forgiving them, and speaking well of them in order to resist the urge to gossip. These will give them reasons to see you as a friend, sister, or brother rather than an enemy.

> On February 2022, *Catholic Update* tells a story of a rabbi who discusses with his disciples the difference between day and night. He asks, "When does the light end and the day begin?" One replies, "Is it the moment when you can tell the difference between a sheep and a dog?" "No," the rabbi answers. Another responds, "Is it when you can tell the difference between a fig tree and an olive tree?" "No," the rabbi says. Then peering deeply into their eyes, he explains,

"It is the moment when you look into the face of your neighbour and recognize her/him as a Sister or Brother. Until that time comes, no matter how bright the day is, it is still night for you." (https://www.liguori.org/).

Incarnational spirituality calls us to forgive. It calls us to see the "other," or our "offender" as our brother or sister who deserves our love and forgiveness, just as God forgives us in love. When we don't forgive, we are in total darkness no matter how bright the day is.

There was a story of a ruthless king who had ten wild dogs. He used them to torture and rip apart those who commit crimes or make mistakes in his kingdom. Forgiveness is not in his vocabulary! The king kept the dogs fierce and hungry by not feeding them well. Once, one of his ministers gave a contrary opinion which he didn't like at all. So, he ordered that the minister be thrown to the dogs. So, the minister beseeched him, "I served you these ten years and you treat me like this? Please give me ten days before you throw me in for the dogs!" Then the king agreed.

For those ten days, the minister befriended the dog keeper and told him that he wants to serve the dogs for the next ten days. The guard hesitated, but he later accepted. The minister began to feed the dogs, clean them, walk them, play with them, and provide all kinds of comfort to them.

Chapter 5: Incarnational Spirituality and Forgiveness

Soon ten days were up, and the king ordered that the minister be thrown in to the dogs for his punishment. But when he was thrown, everyone was surprised at what they saw. They saw the dogs licking the minister's feet! The king was disconcerted by what he saw. He asked, "What happened to the dogs?" The minister then replied, "I served the dogs for only ten days and they have not forgotten my service. Yet, I served you for ten years and you forgot everything at the first mistake." Then the king realized his mistake. He pardoned and ordered the freedom of his minister.

Accessed from https://Saibalsanskaar.wordpress.com

This king learned to temper justice with mercy! He learned to forgive! Forgiveness is designed to set us free. Lewis B. Smedes puts it well: "To forgive is to set a prisoner free, and only to discover that the prisoner was me." Sometimes, we think that by forgiving someone, we are doing that person a favour, and conversely if we don't forgive, that we are keeping them in bondage. The truth is that forgiveness sets us free!

Forgiveness is the only injunction of Jesus that has a condition. "Unless you forgive, you will not be forgiven" (Mt. 6:14-15). It is about not repaying evil for evil. Jesus cautions "Love your enemies, do good to those who hate you, bless those who curse you, pray for those who abuse you" (Lk. 6:27-31). St. Peter writes: "Do not repay evil for evil or abuse for abuse; but, on the contrary, repay with a blessing." (1 Peter 3:8-9). The Book of Sirach (28:2-4) expresses it so well: "Forgive your neighbour the wrong he has done, and then your sins will be pardoned when you pray. Does anyone harbour anger against another and expect healing from the Lord? If people have no mercy toward those like themselves, can they then seek pardon for their own sins?"

These are important questions we need to answer individually! We cannot expect mercy from God when we are not merciful ourselves. We cannot expect healing from God, when we are pouring acids, in form of unforgiveness, into our bodies. C. S. Lewis writes: "To be a Christian means to forgive the inexcusable of others because God has forgiven the inexcusable in you."

In her 2018 TED Talk, Sarah Montana told the story of her journey of forgiveness. When she was 22 years old, her brother and mother were killed during a home break-in. She explained how grief and trauma ate her up for seven years, even though she thought that she had already forgiven the killer. She had told her friends and family that she had forgiven him. She even said: "I forgive you" on national television, and yet she was still wallowing in unforgiveness. She explained: "So if saying you forgive someone is not the same thing as doing it, why was this guy still hooked into my side, dragging me around, making me do dumb things like quitting my job to write a play? It turns out there is no fake it 'till you make it in forgiveness."

After seven years, she wrote to him:

"What happened on December 19th, 2008, was not okay and would probably never be okay for either of us. But just because it wasn't okay, that didn't mean you owed me anything - not an apology, not an explanation, not your role as my villain. I told him that I hated to be reduced to one thing that happened to me one day. I yearned to be more, to be whole, and I didn't think that I could do that if I looked at another person and reduced him to one thing he did one day and made evil the sum of its parts. I told him that I wished him a lifetime full of healing and that I forgave him. And for the first time, there was this lightness of my being."

Forgiveness can take a long time. It is a process and should not be done in a hurry. Sometimes, when we say "I forgive you," we realize that we are still carrying the grief, the anger, and the hurt of unforgiveness. When you experience this, do not be hard on yourself, rather practice self-compassion and self-forgiveness, and little by little through the grace of God you will be set free.

Self-Forgiveness:

How can you forgive others if you do not know how to forgive yourself? Charity, they say, begins at home. We have to begin the process of forgiveness through self-forgiveness. Pope John XXIII once said: "Our lives are messy. Too often, people are unwilling to forgive themselves. Sins weigh heavily; fear and guilt haunt and paralyze." Self-forgiveness is really for the beauty of your soul. It's for your own capacity to feel healed, to be renewed, to let go, to live in love and in a life free from unnecessary baggage that cripples the soul.

Most of us avoid forgiveness like a plague because we do not want to look at our grudges and resentments. Wounds from grudges and rancour are scary; they are downright nasty! It seems better to hold on to it, right? That is why a religious Sister, who had celebrated her sixty years as a nun, held onto a grudge against her Novice Director for over sixty years. When you listen to her, you will hear the same story repeated over and over again. Perhaps, it was a grievous offence and a very grave wound! But to keep it for over sixty years! "Who is suffering?" It is not the Novice Director, of course, because she may not even be aware of the grudge. Like Lazarus in the tomb, this religious sister is still tied to the tomb of unforgiveness. Some of us are still tied to the tomb of past grudges, resentments, anger, hatred, and unforgiveness. This is where Jesus would cry out with a loud voice: "Untie him/her and let him/her go" (Jn. 11:44). Jesus wants to untie us from past hurts and to set us free! We only need to accept the grace and mercy he is offering us and begin with self-forgiveness.

Bhagavad Gita, the Hindu Scripture explains, "If you want to see the brave, look to those who can return love for hatred. If you want to see the heroic, look to those who can forgive." Forgiveness is truly freeing. It's never too late to let go of our villains and reclaim the power we unconsciously give to the monster called unforgiveness. And when we are ready and have made the decision to let go of the bitterness, the pain, the anger, and the malice caused by unforgiveness, we embrace God's grace and freedom.

Many times, we fall into the trap of unforgiveness and lack of compassion, just like the parable of the unforgiven debtor in Mt.

18:23-34 whose huge debts were forgiven, and yet he was not willing to forgive a fellow slave. On the path of unforgiveness, we exhibit apathy, indifference, and lack of concern for others. We force others to pay their debt, but we won't do the same, even though God forgives us no matter how many times we offend him. Jesus preached forgiveness and lived it by asking God to forgive those who crucified him (Lk. 23:34). I am sure that we have the capacity to forgive like Jesus did on the cross! We only need the grace to believe that it is possible even when it is difficult!

The parable of the Prodigal Son, as narrated by Jesus (Lk. 15:11-32) easily comes to mind when we are reflecting on the power of a father's forgiveness. He did not question the demand of the younger son to divide his wealth, but he willingly gave him his share. This is something that is normally done after a father dies, when his children would then divide the inheritance, according to his stipulated will. The "prodigal father," who lavished love, allowed his son to make his own decision. When the son finally decided to return home, his heart was thirsting for the love and forgiveness of his father. He had a rehearsed speech and lists of how to present his case to his father, just as we do when we come before the Lord in prayer! His father did not condemn him! He did not ask what he did with his share of the inheritance, which we would most likely do in a situation like that. We would probably expect this younger son to give an account of what he did with his father's wealth.

Accountability or stewardship is the key! How often do we hold someone by the throat, until they pay through the nose, for what they owe? I wonder what would happen if God treated us the way we treat others! I am not against accountability, but we are called to treat others the way we would love to be treated. That is the Golden Rule! (Mat. 7:12; Lk. 6:31). It is appropriately called the Golden Rule because it encompasses in its few words the underlying and guiding principle of all morality. It also puts vital emphasis on empathy, encouraging us to put ourselves in other's shoes.

Thankfully, this "prodigal father" did not have time for accountability because his love for his children was beyond measure. I imagined him saying: "I am not interested in your rehearsed speech! You are home, that's what matters. Welcome home son, that's where you belong!" The prodigal son's homecoming was more important than the wealth he had squandered. His return home was a sign of love for his family. On the other hand, the older son reacted the way that most of us would, by demanding accountability. He was angry at his father's extravagant love for "this son of his." He never addressed his younger brother as "my brother." He harboured deep seated grudges and saw himself not as "a son," but as a mere slave.

Why did the older son labour like a slave and never even ask for a small goat as a meal, to enjoy with his friends as he claimed? What prevented him from asking? How long did he harbour anger toward his younger brother who was now enjoying what seemed to be his? How many of us get angry when we see God blessing those whom we think should be punished? Did the older son even understand the love his father was offering, or did he only see himself as a labourer? For the younger son: What happened after the celebratory feast? Did he go out to the field the next day as he had promised? This is the kind of story where you get to write your own ending. The ending is your choice! Who do you identify with?

God is always standing by the door, waiting for us to make the decision to return home as did the prodigal son. He is waiting for us to choose to experience His love and see ourselves as children rather than slaves. God loves us unconditionally and wanting only to embrace us with his enormous love. Will you let your God love you? He is always ready to forgive us despite our waywardness. Will you let your God forgive you?

Forgiveness is incarnational! God has taught us to forgive and has called us to live a grudge-free life by forgiving our debtors just as we are forgiven. In fact, there is no authentic living of the incarnational spirituality, if we do not forgive! It makes us more human and more incarnational!

REFERENCES:

C. S. Lewis. (1949). *The Weight of Glory and Other Addresses.* New York: Macmillan Company.

Catholic Update (Feb 2022). "What Did Jesus Mean? Unpacking Gospel Revelations. https://www.liguori.org/

Jack, Kornfield. (2011). "The Ancient Heart of Forgiveness." Mind and Soul Magazine, https://greatergood.berkeley.edu/article/item/the_ancient_heart_of_forgiveness.

McBrien, Richard. (2012). Pope John XXIII's opening address to the Second Vatican Council. Accessed March 7th, 2022, https://www.ncronline.org/blogs/essays-theology/pope-john-xxiiis-opening-address-second-vatican-council

Meenan, John Paul, 2022, The Hope and Forgiveness of Josephine Bakhita, *Catholic Insight.* Accessed May 2022, https://catholic-insight.com/sister-saint-josephine-bakhita-infinite-mercy/

Sarah Montana (2018). Why forgiveness is worth it, Accessed March 7, 2022. https://www.ted.com/talks/sarah_montana_why_forgiveness_is_worth_it?language=en

Chapter 6

Incarnational Spirituality and Religious Community Living

Sr. Patience S. Payne, S.H.F

The Incarnation of Christ is a mystery which explains that Jesus Christ, who is God, took on human flesh and became human like us; he dwelt among us to redeem us. Incarnational spirituality is the state of following Christ's Incarnation and life as a mirror or blueprint, to live out our Christian calling to its full realization in community living.

By looking at Jesus' life, whose incarnational presence is the perfect way of living out our rich diversity in the community, we can clearly see and understand that he took on human flesh out of love, to interact with all humankind and to re-establish that lost relationship between God and his people. Christ was a Jew, but he did not restrict himself solely to the Jewish culture or people. He extended his mission even to the Samaritans and further commissioned us as his followers to go out into the whole world and witness to his incarnational love (Mt. 28:18-20).

This is a shining example that the incarnational spirituality sets before us. It helps us to break down all the barriers that divide and separate people. It allows us to learn and enjoy the richness of each other in our religious communities. For instance, it prompts us to bring to the community our different music, delicacies, arts, recreation, dress, rich cultural practices, stories and folklore, languages, gestures, etc., and thus build and uplift our community life.

What is Religious Community?

Acts of the Apostles 2:42-47 defines what a religious community is: "Day by day, the apostles devoted themselves to teaching and fellowship, to the breaking of bread and prayers. Awe came upon everyone because many wonders and signs were done by the apostles. All who believed were together and had all things in common." The word community is from a Latin word—communitas. "Com" literally means with/together; and "munus" means gift. This suggests that a community is a small social unit that shares similar values and gifts.

According to *Vita Consecrata* (# 42), "A community life is a life that is shared in love…among the consecrated persons, who become of one heart and soul (Acts 4:32), through the love poured into their hearts by the Holy Spirit, (Rm. 5:5), and who experienced an interior call to share everything in common." Religious community that is embedded in incarnational spirituality is a community of people who share a common goal, vision, constitution, and mission together according to the spirituality and charism of their founder in accordance with the Gospel values of love, compassion, forgiveness, kindness, and hospitality.

A religious community is a home where a group of religious people live together. These religious people share a feeling of fellowship with one another because of sharing common interests, gifts, spirituality, charism, and goals. No religious person can live the vows effectively outside of the community because these evangelical counsels bind the community members together. Can. 665 explains that "each religious is to reside in their own religious house and observe the common life." One cannot observe the vows of poverty, chastity, and obedience by living alone. It is in the community that we live out these vows through service to one another, through obedience to the authorities, loving, and sharing things in common through the vow of poverty.

It is in God that we see a perfect communion life. God is a Trinitarian God and a communion of Persons, simultaneously distinct and perfectly united in love. The Trinitarian God created humans in his image and likeness (Gn 1:26-27) for communion. No one is an island, and we need each other in a community of love. We are called by God to enter an intimate relationship with Him, and to live interpersonal communion with each other. However, this is not always the case because of our fallen human nature. After the fall, God expressed his love for us through the mystery of the Incarnation. Jesus became human in order to share his life with us and reconcile us with God. Thus, we become children of God and co-heirs with Christ (Rm. 8:17).

Our rich diversity serves as an eye opener that encourages innovation, promotes and awakens creativity, and enhances the sharing of knowledge and ideas. A story is told about a community of sisters who came from different ethnic backgrounds but lived in one community. A few of the sisters looked down on one particular sister because she came from a very poor country. This sister was very good with music and the liturgy, but because of their biases, they could neither enjoy her musical gifts nor make use of them in adding life to their community prayers. That sister was later missioned to another community where her gift of music was appreciated. Her community's liturgy of the Holy Hours and the Eucharist became very lively and a beautiful celebration of God's love.

In another community, a group of sisters decided to incorporate the various cultures of their diverse members in their community living. For instance, their menu includes food from different cultures, their convents have artifacts from the countries of their sisters, and they learned the music in the local languages of some members and use them during their prayers. Everybody in that community feels represented to some degree, and that brings about a sense of belonging.

Our rich diversity should enable us to enjoy and appreciate the vast variety of our community members and use all its richness to accomplish our common goal and further the mission of Christ, rather than to tear each other down. That is why François-Marie Arouet, popularly known as Voltaire, expressed that Religious Community is "People who come together without knowing each other, live together without loving each other, and die without regretting each other" (Brocard, Sewell. 1970, P 146). We should ask ourselves if there is some truth in his statement. Was he totally wrong?

It is evident that community living comes with different challenges. The fact is that we as community members, most often come from different countries, backgrounds, upbringings, cultural settings, etc., and our rich diversity can become a huge challenge if we do not manage and utilize it appropriately. Very often, instead of our rich diversity becoming a source of strength and resource, it turns into a means of division and separates us even more. That is why incarnational spirituality should be the root value of our community life. It means that we are to have hearts of flesh rather than stone (Ezek. 36:26). Since people usually frown at or shy away from what they do not know or understand, there is one particular congregation that makes it a tradition at every general gathering for one sister to share her cultural background. This has helped most of the sisters come to know and appreciate the cultures of their fellow sisters better, so that there is more understanding and acceptance among them.

We are called to harness these differences to our greatest advantage and for our common growth in carrying out our mission. Our uniqueness should not become stumbling blocks in the realization of our collective goals/charism. Our community life calls us for a prayerful presence: Not only physical presence, but also mental, spiritual, affective, and fraternal presence: "How wonderful it is for God's people to dwell together in love" (Ps. 133:1).

Sometimes, we are so busy in our communities that we don't see the tears in our sister's/brother's eyes. Very often we are not sensitive to the silent voice that seeks our attention. Community life, lived in the spirit of incarnational spirituality, calls us to actively participate in the lives of the community members. This means being sensitive to one another's needs, along with mutual respect, love, and trust. It advocates for the zeal of pursuing a common interest and goal through the charism and spirit of the founders/foundresses.

Incarnational community living is the ability to enjoy as well as embrace our rich diversity in a community setting, as we selflessly assume roles and responsibilities for the benefit of others. This requires complete humility which will enable us to step out of our comfort zones for the common good. It also involves entering the history/culture/lifestyle of others with the mind set of understanding it, giving it life and meaning, and clothing it with positivity for happy community living. It calls us to set aside our biases, prejudices, envies, and negative attitudes toward differences, and instead embrace peace, mutual sensitivity, understanding, and compassion toward one another.

Incarnational community living calls for the mending of broken relationships and reconciliation between community members. This can be made possible by showing these people the unconditional love and Divine mercy of our God. This kind of community relationship prompts us to bring people closer to God by recreating a concrete relationship between God and his people, and by the tangible gift of ourselves in the service of God and others. Community living affords us the opportunity to live out our spirituality in an authentic way, and Christ is the perfect model in genuinely living out what we call a life-giving community.

In summary, we should remember that the incarnational community and spirituality is rooted and grounded in God's love for us, and this demands that we show practical and tangible love for one another in our religious communities. That is why incarnational spirituality moves and motivates us to selflessly live out God's love in a very concrete way.

As Catherine Doherty puts it: "Christians are called to become icons of Christ and to reflect Him. We are called to incarnate Christ in our lives, to clothe our lives with Him, so that people can see Him in us, touch Him in us, and recognize Him in us."

REFERENCES:

Brocard, Sewell. *The Vatican Oracle,* California, USA: Duckworth, 1970, P 146.

Doherty, Catherine. (1995). *The Gospel Without Compromise.* Ontario, Canada: Madonna House Publications.

Pope John Paul II, *Vita Consecrata,* March 25, 1996 (Accessed May 31, 2022). https://www.vatican.va/content/john-paul-ii/en/apost_exhortations/documents/hf_jp-ii_exh_25031996_vita-consecrata.html

Chapter 7

Embodying the Love of the Incarnate Word in Intercultural and Intergenerational Religious Communities

Sr. Adaku H. Ogbuji, CCVI

"If I don't have a home in my religious community, I will look for it outside of the community," said a religious person in one of the workshops I gave. Among the basic human needs are feeling the sense of belonging and being accepted; to love and to be loved. When these needs are not met in our religious communities, then they are sought from outside. We live with people of different cultures, generations, races, nationalities, educational backgrounds, ethnic groups, and languages in our respective religious communities. As such, we are called to build a home where all can live, and everyone feels accepted, loved, and respected. This is the greatest treasure of being human: the ability and capacity to give and receive love, as well as to spread love in our world. Because of our diversities, we are different and unique in the way we love, think, do things, communicate, assimilate information, greet, sing, dress, hug, shake hands, eat, and even pray. Because of our cultural differences, intercultural sensitivity and receptivity are values we need in our religious communities.

We are required to hold each other's hand, care for, and be kind to each other in our intercultural communities. The holding of hands is sometimes very challenging. Some hands are difficult to hold, others are very easy, and still others are neither difficult nor easy, but indifferent. As humans, we are inclined to "hold the hands" of those we love and relate better with, rather than those we dislike. In other words, we avoid/isolate personalities that we dread, but relate better with personalities that are less threatening to us. God, in His infinite mercy, holds the hands of each of us individually and with much love, no matter how difficult or headstrong we tend to be. God's compassion falls on everyone, no matter how much we turn our backs on God. It reminds me of an anecdote: One day a man was crossing a bridge in life but was scared. So, he turned and asked God: "Can I hold your hand so that I may not fall?" God responded: "No, my child, I will hold your hand." He asked, "What is the difference?" God replied, "If you hold my hand and something happens, you might let go. But if I hold your hand, no matter what happens, I will never let you go." Intercultural living, in religious communities, requires us to hold each other's hands, no matter how difficult it might be.

Religious communities are designated homes for consecrated men and women, who are guided by a certain way of life, common spirituality, the charism of their founder, and who live out their vowed life by sharing things in common (Ogbuji, 2019). A religious person, according to the Canon Law is a man or woman who is consecrated by the profession of the evangelical counsels of poverty, chastity, and obedience. One who follows Christ more closely under the action of the Holy Spirit and is totally dedicated to God who is loved most of all, for the up-building of the Church and the salvation of the world (Can. 573, #1). Religious people are human beings with flaws and imperfections, who are striving for holiness.

Chapter 7: Embodying the Love of the Incarnate Word

In their imperfections, they make mistakes and bad choices. They are also unique and different in their personalities and the way they live out their vowed life. As such, it is both a challenge as well as a gift to live out these differences in our various religious communities, given the fact that sometimes we don't get to choose with whom to live.

God creates differences; therefore, difference is good. But sometimes it is not very pleasant to be different. And, of course, having a different passport is not so nice in some countries; sometimes, you are kept waiting in the line for a longer time. We only need to respect and accept our differences and commit to a world that is less violent and less racist. It is good to ask ourselves: Are we aware of the way we treat those who are different from us, especially those whose hands we have difficulty holding? We can learn from others when we learn the dignity of difference (Anthony Gittins, *Living Mission Interculturally*, 2015).

To value the dignity of difference, it is essential and crucial that we embody the love of the Incarnate Word in our intercultural and intergenerational communities. Incarnating our differences means that we are genuinely respecting and appreciating the "other." We appreciate and treat the other with dignity and love so that they feel at home in the community. Incarnating our differences also calls us to hold each other's hands and walk together as the Synodal process beckons us, not walking in front or behind, but walking side by side.

On Oct. 10, 2021, Pope Francis formally opened a two-year process called "a synod on synodality," officially known as "Synod

2021-2023: For a Synodal Church." During these years and beyond, we are called to walk together as a Church with the Holy Spirit guiding us in communion, participation, and mission. We can pause and ask ourselves: Are we really walking together? Are there some members of our congregations who are left behind? Are there no members of our respective congregations who are walking in front so that others would follow, maybe because they are the dominant culture? How is this "walking together" manifesting in our intercultural and intergenerational religious communities?

What is Intercultural Living?

Interculturality is different from internationality. When people from different cultures or nationalities live together, it does not necessarily suggest that they are living interculturally. Also, when religious people live in an international community, it is not a guarantee that they are living interculturally. Intercultural living is a theological word which depicts people of different cultures trying to intentionally live out a common faith (Gittins, 2015). It is an act of faith that opens us to a new path of evangelization and authentic witness to the gospel that Jesus preached (Acts 11: 26). Intercultural living is expressed by people of different cultures coming together to build a new community, a new home where every member finds a place and yet no one is privileged above anyone else. Each person, in effect, leaves their primary or original home in order to come together and build a new home from the fabric of each person's life and culture (Gittings, 2015).

Intercultural living demands graciousness, diplomacy, listening heart, mutual respect, serious dialogue, open/transparent communication without judgment, and the development of a common and sustaining vision. It is not enough to tolerate each other's unique food, language, arts, or observe a national holiday for a particular culture in a community. Intercultural living goes beyond these gestures. A daily conversion is a vital attitude; intercultural sensitivity, storytelling, and commitment are required to sustain this faith-based undertaking. Storytelling is absolutely necessary in understanding cultural differences.

What is culture?

Culture is specific to humans. Animals are not cultured; rather, they have instinct and can learn particular behaviors. Culture gives us identity and a sense of belonging. It is a way of life that is learned and becomes a part of us, and we in turn teach others consciously and unconsciously. People reflect their cultural values, beliefs, principles, ethics, ideologies, symbols, norms, rituals, and heritages and live them out consciously and unconsciously without thinking. Culture is symbolic and dynamic; consequently, understanding of culture is intimately related to the understanding of what it means to be human. It reflects in the way we speak, interpret symbols, in languages, arts, stories, music, rituals, and we do transmit them from one generation to another. For instance, respect for elders: I find it very difficult to call my elder Sisters by their first names because it is not appropriate in my culture. I found it difficult also to interrupt my teacher when he/she is still speaking. I had to raise my hand until he/she saw my raised hand. On the contrary, my classmates from the United States would just chip in during a class conversation when they had a question.

Some cultures are flexible with time. When an event is scheduled for 9:00 am, some people start showing up an hour late and then the event may also begin an hour later. Sometimes, the meaning of a word is different: e.g., brother and sister do not necessarily mean siblings in some cultures. Maintaining eye contact is encouraged and considered as a sign of respect in one culture (low context culture), while in another culture, it is disrespectful (high context culture). Similarly, in low context culture, the communication pattern is direct while it is indirect in high context culture (Edward T Hall, 1977, *Beyond Culture,* Anchor Books). None of this is superior to the other; they are simply different ways to relay information.

In conversation, sometimes we falsely assume what is said without seeking clarification. We invent and make up what we think is missing in the story, which is mostly inaccurate. The worst mistake is that we think we know the communicator's intention. Remember that intention is invisible to the eyes! Sometimes, people act with mixed intention, others with no intention, and others with a good intention. The way we communicate and interpret what is communicated is rooted in our unconscious cultural heritage. Thus, accepting our cultural differences and asking questions for clarity are imperative in intercultural living, rather than judging, false assumption, and/or putting people down.

I have lived in several intercultural communities as a Catholic Religious Sister, and I am still living and enjoying my life in an intercultural/intergenerational community. From experience, I recognized that intercultural living is both life-giving and challenging. It is beautiful to live with Sisters from different cultures, where we share our gifts in order to enrich our religious communities. It is at the same time challenging to feel and experience the pain of cultural misunderstanding, use of belittling or derogatory words, as well as bias in religious communities. The most painful aspect of living interculturally for me was the experiences of unconscious bias and comments that evidently depict discrimination and derogation. I visited a religious community of sisters one day, and I decided to make some pancakes for them for breakfast. After the sisters had finished enjoying my pancakes, one of them asked me: "Helen, do you eat pancakes in Africa?" Firstly, I was disappointed that this sister had just finished enjoying my pancakes. Did it not occur to her that I knew how to make pancakes before I joined religious life? Secondly, Africa is a continent of 54 countries, and not a single country.

Sometimes, we play the "victims of ignorance" when we think of Africa as a country. In Nigeria alone, which is my country, there are 371 ethnic groups with different cultures and different ways of doing things. I was only formed by one culture, and I am ignorant of the cultures of the other 370 groups in Nigeria. If it is very unfair and impossible to box all these ethnic groups in Nigeria into one culture, how much more the other 53 countries in the African continent! Because ignorance of the law is no excuse, therefore, ignorance of our cultural bias is no excuse!

Culture impacts who we are, as well as how we behave/relate and communicate! We bring these values to religious life and live them out unconsciously on a daily basis. We wear cultural lenses that are different and unique, which sometimes lead to bias, ethnocentrism, and cultural blindness. Ethnocentrism simply means the act of judging another culture based on the standard of our own culture. The questions to ask ourselves are: Am I interested and curious to know the cultures of the people I live with? Can I relax easily with other cultures and even become attracted to their way of doing things without judgment? Am I open to building relationships, enjoying being around and interacting with other cultures? What cultural lens do I wear? How does my lens affect or cloud the way I see myself and others?

Each of us sees things from our own cultural lens, and we are clouded by our cultural values. Some cultures like to shake hands while greeting, others bow, others prostrate on the floor, others kneel, and others hug. None of this is better than another. Although different and unique, they communicate the same thing: "I greet you!" If I am wearing red spectacles, everything will look red; and I will perceive issues from that viewpoint. The same with green or any other color. None of this is better; it is just different and unique color! It is the same with cultural lenses!

We are all humanized by the society and the culture into which we are born. Nobody knows completely what the real world is, but everyone does know the world from their own culture. Sometimes, we begin to look at people and judge them from our own cultural values. This leads to bias, prejudices, and ethnocentric behavior, or even racial discrimination. We all are somewhat ethnocentric because we love our way of doing things, and we think it is the best, so we judge people according to our own values and cultures.

Chapter 7: Embodying the Love of the Incarnate Word

Some people are judged by their skin color, physical appearance, or by their accent. A German was once shocked because a black man could communicate in the German language.

Ethnocentrism starts with denial, sometimes we defend our denial, and other times we minimize the damage it is causing. Denial or ignorance of our racial bias or ethnocentrism is not an excuse! When we treat people in our congregations differently because of their skin color or where they come from, we are not authentic witnesses to the gospel. How do we celebrate feast days/birthdays in our religious communities? Are there some community members whose feast days are flamboyantly celebrated with great meals, while others are not even remembered or sometimes celebrated quietly? A religious sister once called me and said: "Today is my feast day and nobody, in the community, seems to remember it. Last month we celebrated Sr. Greeks' feast day, we decorated the house with beautiful signs and prepared delicious meals. But today, nobody thought about me."

How do we welcome new members to our communities? Do we use two different measures depending on where they come from? Do we use an assimilation process? She/he has to become one of us! The community does not need to change, but the new members must change! Those who resist change are marginalized or removed! In this model, potential members are effectively invited to join a pre-existing, well-established community by learning its history, structures, and practices, and becoming assimilated into it. This community might be most welcoming and hospitable, showing the newcomers how things are done and should be done, but the personal wishes and cultural traditions of the incoming member are of little or no account. If a person was deemed to be sufficiently able to assimilate into the community, all would be well (Gittings, 2015).

Gittings continued: "This assimilation model must move to mutual welcome and ultimately to radical welcome where people bring their cultural values to form new homes of religious communities, a home of intercultural sensitivity and inclusion." Intercultural sensitivity is the ability to develop a positive attitude toward understanding and caring for cultural differences, and acceptance of other cultures. Similarly, radical welcome is also called radical hospitality, and it is a practice of putting extraordinary effort and emphasis on making community members feel welcome. It focuses on breaking down barriers that prevent people from participating actively in communities or feeling at home. The questions we can ask ourselves are: Have we moved to a radical inclusion in our intercultural communities? Are we just trying to coexist rather than discovering how each member's personal transformation can lead both to mutual enrichment and the transformation of a whole community? Every culture requires transformation and conversion. No culture is perfect, and every culture is limited by space and time. Jesus was not an exception! He went through a cultural conversion as seen in the story of the Canaanite woman (Mt. 15:21-28) and the Samaritan Woman at the Well (Jn.4:1-42). In the same way, we are called to a daily cultural conversion!

Chapter 7: Embodying the Love of the Incarnate Word

The Stories of the Cultural Conversion of Jesus and the Apostles:

Jesus, as a faithful Jew, was shaped by his cultural values and norms. As a Jew, he may have prayed the prayer of the male Jews; i.e., thanking God that he was born a Jew not a Gentile; and also, a man and not a woman (Ogbuji, 2021). It is not surprising that when Jesus sent the twelve apostles out on a mission in Mt. 10:5-6, he told them to go only to the lost sheep of the house of Israel. He himself confessed it as well: "I was sent only to the lost sheep of the house of Israel" (Mt. 15:24). How was Jesus able to change from an ethnocentric mentality (Mt. 10:5; Mt. 15:21-28) to a more inclusive approach for the gentiles?

The ethnocentric attitude of Jesus was very apparent in the healing story of the Canaanite Woman's daughter in Matthew 15:21-28. She was a foreigner and a gentile. She was called names (dog), a racial insult. When Jesus told the woman, "It is not fair to take the children's bread and throw it to the dogs." The response of the woman was powerful: "Yes, Lord, yet even the dogs eat the crumbs that fall from their master's table." With the woman's response, Jesus for once, loses his argument and opens up to the "other," the "stranger," and to the "different" (Ogbuji, 2021). This was an Aha! Moment for Jesus. It was a moment of intercultural conversion. Jesus embraces the challenge and changes to the radical inclusion of everyone.

During his public ministry, Jesus gathered around him the marginalized, sinners, women, and tax collectors in his table fellowship. After his ascension, the disciples continued in his mission. But they, too, as Jewish people, were prejudiced against the gentiles. St. Peter's first cultural conversion took place in the house of Cornelius. Acts 10:9-15, 34-35 recounted how in the dream, Peter was asked to kill and eat the animals he regarded as unclean, and he responded in the negative saying, "I will not!" Then God told him not to call any created thing unclean. After this trance, God sent him to the house of a Gentile, Cornelius. Here, Peter realized that no one should call anyone unclean and that God has no favorite.

Peter was rebuked by the Church in Jerusalem for going to the house of Cornelius, the uncircumcised, and dined with them (Acts 11:3). But Peter defended his stand (Acts 11:17): "Who was I to stand in the way of God?" Another encounter of Peter's ethnocentrism was when Paul rebuked him for his hypocritical and insincere attitude toward the Gentiles in Galatians 2:11-21. Peter was eating with the uncircumcised believers until some circumcised party, who came from James arrived, Peter separated himself from them. Paul reproached Peter's ethnocentric attitude saying: "If you, though a Jew, live like a Gentile, how can you compel the Gentiles to live like Jews." After all these discriminations and prejudices, the Council in Jerusalem made a decision: "We ought not to cause God's Gentile converts any difficulties" (Acts 15:14-19). This was a cultural conversion for the followers of Jesus.

No culture is perfect; therefore, the theology of intercultural living calls us to daily conversion, and to consciously live out our faith in the context of our culture knowing that we are one in the Lord. It has a Trinitarian foundation because of the unity in the

Chapter 7: Embodying the Love of the Incarnate Word

Triune God. It also has a theological foundation because Jesus prayed for our unity saying, "Father, that they all may be one" (Jn.17:21). St. Paul reiterated the same truth in Gal. 3:28 when he said: "There is neither Jew nor Greek, there is neither slave nor free, there is neither male nor female; for you are all one in Christ Jesus." Our religious communities will become incarnational communities when we internalize this truth. We will be transformed by each member's talent and faith commitment, rather than competing among ourselves. Interculturality is a GIFT! Apart from the gifts of intercultural living, there is also the gift of intergenerational living in our religious communities.

Intergenerational Religious Living

During our November 2-7, 2021, Religious Formation Conference in the United States through the zoom, one of the topics discussed was the issue of intergenerational living in religious life entitled: "In Their Own Words: Wisdom for Formators from Newer Members." Sisters Mary Pat Garvin, (RSM) and Michelle Lesher, (SSJ) both described the frustration of the newer members when it comes to enjoying religious life in intergenerational communities. One question that was asked really stood out for me: How can we better serve our newest members in a life-giving community? All the formators present at the conference listened to the experiences of the newer members to religious life.

One person expressed: "The energy of the novice is circumvented by the tired nature of many communities…Our Congregation seems to be far more focused on the realities of our older and aging sisters rather than our newest members. How do we find a balance?"

Another person stated: "Most religious congregations struggle to offer a healthy local community for second-year novices and temporary professed sisters. There are fewer sisters, many live alone, others are not open to welcoming a woman in formation in their community, or the dynamics within the community aren't healthy…It is frustrating to be taught a lot of theories around conflict management, intimacy, and theology of religious life, and then be placed in a local community as a second-year novice where those skills are not practiced with Sisters in their fifties, sixties and above. This is the circumstance I found myself in and it has brought me a lot of sadness, disappointments, and confusion. Is the religious life I'm discerning the ideal that I was taught in the canonical novitiate or the actuality that I lived as a second-year novice in the local community?" (Sr. Lesher's Presentation).

During this conference, it was very obvious that the younger generation are looking for a vibrant community, and the older members desire to have the younger members join their communities. However, it is difficult sometimes for both the older and newer members to find a common ground of relationality. The younger generation has a lot of energy and love the older sisters, and the older sisters also love them, but are afraid to stretch. How do we balance or put into rhythm the energy and vulnerability of both the newer and older members?

What is Intergenerational Living?

Every congregation is made up of members of different generational cohorts. A generational cohort is a group of people who are born approximately within the ages of 15-20 years span (Garvin, 2021). Each cohort shares certain formative developmental experiences such as the composition of family of origin, cultural values, the type of education received, different forms of entertainment, etc. These attributes shape the worldview and beliefs of each cohort. However, two individuals from the same cohort could still be unique while also sharing much in common because of environmental factors.

Intergenerational living is where we find two or more generational cohorts living together in religious communities: For instance, the Silent generation (1928-45), Baby boomers (1946-64), generation X (1965-80), and generation Y or Millennials (1981-96) may be living together as community members. Because each cohort has different formative orientation, different family orientation, and work attitudes, it can bring misunderstanding and apprehension of one generation toward another.

The silent generation values a strong nuclear family and discipline. They use letters in communicating, and for them work is a privilege. Their leadership style is command and control, authority is to be respected. They were affected by World War II; thus, they experienced the Great Depression, and they grew up rationing food. The baby boomers value stay-at-home moms and are more competitive in the work environment. They are optimistic, very involving, independent, and self-assured. Generation X are individualistic, flexible, and technologically skillful. They value work and are loyal to their profession but balance it with leisure. They use email and cell phones to communicate, and there is an increase in single parent homes among this generation.

Generation Y grew up with technology such as the Internet, computers, video games, and social media, but they are consumed by social media. They are more globally-minded than previous generations and are more accepting of differences in race, gender, sexual orientation, and ethnicity. They live with parents who exert control over them and the issues of separation and divorce in families affect them. They prefer mobile working, and they rely on technology. Generation Z lacks "face to face" relationships due to the extensive use of smartphones and social media. They mostly suffer loneliness, anxiety, and fragility. However, they are compassionate, thoughtful, open-minded, responsible, and determined to succeed. They are more independent, confident, and autonomous than previous generations.

With the above information, we can speculate the differences in each cohort and how living with different generations can be both a graced community and a challenge. Just as an individual joins religious congregation with his/her cultural lens, so also does each generational cohort come with their own particular lens. It is worthy to note that a person who has come into our community has come either to teach us something, or to learn something from us. Hence, the community members have some work to do in order to make their community a home. They must develop the ability to listen with their hearts and learn from each other. Often, we are too busy to notice the needs of our community members, other times we are in a hurry to do our daily chores and ministry so that we don't "hear the cry of the poor" in our communities. This reminds me of a story about a father who happened to be a workaholic.

> One evening his four-year-old son approached him and asked, "Dad, how much do you make in an hour?" The Dad was surprised at the question and also felt uncomfortable. He responded, "Son, why do you ask? Even your mother doesn't know how much I make in an hour. Go to bed, it is late." The son went off to bed angry that his question had not been answered and laid there on his back staring up at the ceiling. After a few minutes, the father felt bad at the way he had dismissed his little son. He went to his room and sat down on the side of his bed. "Son, I am sorry for the way I answered you. To tell you the truth, I only make twenty dollars per hour." The son answered, "Can I have ten out of your twenty dollars?" The father hesitated a moment, and then went to his room to get the money and bring it back to his son. He couldn't help wondering what all this drama was about. His son reached under his pillow, pulled out a ten-dollar bill, added it to the one his father had just given him and said: "Dad, here is twenty dollars. Can I buy an hour of your time?" His father was dumbfounded, but from that moment onwards, he knew what had to be done.

Intergenerational living requires sensitivity to the needs of every member, open-mindedness to what is new, and patience for this journey of inclusivity. The community should be open to dance to the rhythm of balancing the diminishing energy of the older community members, with the energy and vibrant nature of the younger members.

Fr. Anthony de Mello, SJ, once told a story of a young girl who joined a cloistered congregation. She brought much joy and energy to the community of older nuns. At some point, she thought that her energy was no longer bringing life and joy to the community. She started questioning her vocation and began to feel lonely. One of the older nuns noticed that her energy was going down, so she embarked on more prayers for her, asking God to save her vocation in their convent. But none of the nuns expressed to her how much they appreciated her joy and energy in the community. Finally, the young nun left the convent thinking that she was never wanted. The older nun who had been praying blamed God for not answering her prayers and recounted her experience to her spiritual director. The spiritual director admonished her not to blame God because she never affirmed the goodness in this younger sister, who just needed a word of affirmation from her community members.

While some newer members enjoy the wisdom from the older community members, others find their lack of energy and enthusiasm a challenge. According to Sr. Michelle Lesher (2018),

> People often ask if I ever hesitated in joining an Order where there are more wisdom figures than peers. The truth

is, I didn't notice because I was too busy being inspired by these women who were living a life that matched the one to which I felt called. These women are my mentors and sisters. I am increasingly amazed to find that despite having grown up in different times, our stories about feeling compelled by religious life are remarkably similar. When we talk about matters of the heart and what is central to our religious life—relationship with God and service to our dear neighbor—age isn't all that significant. I felt drawn to the mission of the Sisters of Saint Joseph and questions around age never deter that call.

For an intergenerational community to be healthy, the members must be willing to learn from each other. This relational learning requires that individuals be both grounded and flexible; capable of listening to one's own desires and those of other community members (Garvin, 2021). Therefore, there is a need for respect, authenticity, cooperation, mutual support, forbearance, tolerance, and humility. There is also a need for members of an intergenerational community to be able to offer and receive challenges. Embracing our differences with a sense of joy and gratitude can make a difference in our communities.

There is also a need for intergenerational solidarity (Garvin, 2021). According to Pope Francis: "Intergenerational solidarity is not optional, but rather a basic question of justice, since the world we have received also belongs to those who will follow us" (Laudato Si #159). Pope Francis reiterated in his TED Talk delivered from the Vatican City on April 25, 2017: "Let us help each other, all together, to remember that the 'other' is not a statistic, or a number. We all need each other." When we help each other, it will bring a sense of belonging to the members, intimacy, a healthy community living, and amicable conflict resolution.

What defines being human is the capacity to give and receive love, and what is most important in our intergenerational and intercultural communities is to embody and spread this love in our world. The possible way of expressing this love is unique to each one of us and each of us are an expression of God's love. Thus, we are a gift to our religious communities rather than a problem. Sometimes, we view the "other" as a problem or a challenge to live with. But in the actual sense, it might reflect what is inside of us—our shadows. A wise saying has it: "I find what I look for in people. If I look for God, I find God. If I look for bad qualities, I find them." And this reminds me of the story of the echo of life:

> A son and his father were walking on the mountains. Suddenly, the son falls, hurts himself and screams: "AAAhhhhhhhh!!!" To his surprise, he hears the voice repeating, somewhere in the mountain: "AAAhhhhhhh!!!" Curious, he yells: "Who are you?" He receives the answer: "Who are you?" Angered at the response, he screams: "Coward!" He receives the answer: "Coward!" He looks to his father and asks: "What's going on?" The father smiles and says: "My son, pay attention." And then he screams to the mountain: "I admire you!" The voice answers: "I admire you!" Again, the man screams: "You are a champion!"

> The voice answers: "You are a champion!" The boy is surprised but does not understand. Then the father explains: "People call this ECHO, but really this is LIFE. It gives you back everything you say or do. Our life is simply a reflection of our actions. If you want more love in the world, create more love in your heart. Life will give you back everything you have given to it. (Author Unknown)

Yes, if we want more love, we have to give it. The more we give, the more we will receive. And the Holy Scripture says: We will reap what we sow (Gal. 6:8). What is in your heart when you relate with people who are different from you? Do you see God or your shadow? When real inclusion is practiced and each community member is mutually enriched by the new way of living the faith, we will enter the culture of one another with respect, dialogue, sensitivity, compassion, and vulnerability. We will remove our culture-colored lenses, prejudices, and biases in order to clearly and genuinely embody the love of the Incarnate Word in our intercultural and intergenerational religious communities. We will walk together as synodal Church!

References:

Gittings, A. J. & Arbuckle, G. A., (2015). *Living Mission Interculturally: Faith, Culture, and the Renewal of Praxis.* Collegeville, MN: Liturgical Press.

Lesher, M. (2018). The Passion of Youth Meets the Wisdom of Age. *VISION: A Resource of the National Religious Vocation*

Conference. https://vocationnetwork.org/en/articles/show/605-the-passion-of-youth-meets-the-wisdom-of-age

Ogbuji, A. H. (2021). *Out of the Lips of Infants, Wisdom Comes: Retelling the Bible Stories.* Nairobi, Kenya: Franciscan Kolbe Press.

Pope Francis (2017). "Why the Future Worth Building Includes Everyone." TED Talk. Accessed, https://www.ted.com/talks/his_holiness_pope_francis_why_the_only_future_worth_building_includes_everyone?language=en

Chapter 8

Attitudes and Dispositions for Incarnational Formative Process

Fr. Remigius Ikpe (O.C.D.)

One of the fundamental human rights that we all possess is the right to human dignity. Dignity is the right of a person to be valued and respected for their own sake. There is also the right to love and to be loved. The attitude and dispositions of incarnational formative process point to these rights. This disposition refers to an experience of formation that helps the candidate to encounter the redeeming, saving, and sanctifying ministry of Jesus Christ in the formator and the formation process. When the process of formation is incarnational in nature, it helps the candidate in formation to feel at "home" as he/she perceives the Incarnate Word in the life and actions of the formator. A closer examination of the document issued by the Congregation for Institutes of Consecrated Life and Societies of Apostolic Life, on *Directives on Formation in Religious Institutes* in 1990, reveals some of the attitudes and dispositions for an incarnational formative experience. This chapter explores the attitudes and dispositions recommended by this document of the Church for an effective approach to formation that reveals the Incarnate Word to the candidate.

A very touching experience was narrated about a candidate who went to the formator to ask for money in order to bind his thesis that he needed to submit for school. The formator did not hesitate in giving the money that was requested because a bound thesis was a requirement of the school program. However, the student had exaggerated the amount because he had planned to use the extra to entertain his friends at a bar. He had been joining his group of friends in drinking beer and up until then they had always provided the drink. Now, it was his turn to buy the beer, but he did not know how to ask for the beer money from his formator, so he added it to the amount needed for the binding of the thesis.

Everything went well, and he invited his friends to the usual bar, and they all praised and hailed him and began their celebration. However, as chance may have it, his formator happened to be passing through that area and was surprised to see his brother in a beer parlor, drinking with friends. When he glanced at the place, his eyes happened to meet the eyes of the candidate, after which he walked away quickly because he did not want to spoil the good time they were having. However, the celebration was already spoiled because the candidate noticed that his formator had seen him. From that time on, the drink tasted like paint and glue. He was sure that he had gotten himself into trouble.

When he arrived at the community in the evening, he attended the prayer like every other candidate but with fear in his heart. He could not eat his supper. He was sure that he was going to be summoned for dismissal. But to his great surprise, nothing happened. Everything went on as usual until the end of the month, when the candidates were supposed to go for consultation/accompaniment with the formator. On that fateful day, he presented himself as usual, talking about his prayer life, community experience, studies, apostolate, and his relationship with others, etc., according to the guideline for spiritual accompaniment. Everything was excellent because he was really a very committed and generous candidate. The formator was impressed with his efforts and praised him for them.

When the accompaniment session was over, this candidate stepped out of the accompaniment room feeling dissatisfied and heavily burdened because the formator had neither addressed the issue of exaggerating the amount for binding his thesis, nor his drinking with his friends without permission. He went back to the accompaniment room and nervously asked the formator if they had really met. The formator responded in the affirmative: "Of course, we just finished an accompaniment session with you." He then asked the formator: "But you did not ask me about it." To which the formator responded: "But you did not talk about it." At that stage, there was a deep silence, and the tension in the candidate was so overwhelming that he did not know what to say. The formator then looked at him and gently said, "Go, I understand." The candidate heaved a sigh of relief as if a big load was taken off his mind. That was a moment of deep healing, a compassionate, and an incarnational encounter with the candidate.

"Go, I understand!" It is like saying to him: "Go and sin no more." "Go, your sins are forgiven." The formator did not scream at him or call him names. He didn't condemn, judge, or threaten him as the one who would determine his fate during ordination or profession of vows. This was an incarnational experience of a formative process that made a profound impact in the life of this candidate, to the extent that he remembered it with nostalgia. This candidate was the Provincial Superior of his Congregation when he shared this story with a group of formators. This story points to the type of attitude and disposition that the Church encourages formators to have so that candidates in the formative process in religious life may encounter Christ, the Incarnate Word, in the formator's life and in their formation process.

There are certain principles that are required in an incarnational formative process: The first principle is a disposition and an attitude that recognizes in the candidates the inviolable human value that the candidate possesses as a human person made in the image and likeness of God. This attitude and disposition would enable a formator to recognize the inviolable human dignity of a candidate and approach the candidate with unconditional positive regard, with respect, and with compassion. This first principle is foundational for understanding the mystery of the incarnation and Jesus' life, ministry, suffering, and death for the salvation of the human race.

Respect for this principle of inviolable human value helps the formator to be in touch with the mandate that he or she has to lead the candidate out of their low human conditions of life and into a life of grace. This however does not contradict the fact that there are prerequisites for authentic vocation to the consecrated life. This principle does not mean that everyone has the required potential to live a consecrated life. Rather, it calls for discernment, but with the principle that the candidate has an inviolable human value, even when they need to be discontinued for a lack of positive indicators to the vocation of a religious life.

The second principle is that vocation is a gift of God which the candidates are helped to develop, and not an innate personal quality to be discovered. This principle or disposition helps the formator to embrace the work of instilling values and helping the candidates to develop such gifts as generosity, creativity, and an inclusive love for the Incarnate Word. This is one of the main reasons why the document mentioned above strongly emphasized that: "The proper renewal of religious institutes depends chiefly on the formation of their members. Consecrated life, whether in the Diocesan setting or in Religious Institutes, brings together disciples of Christ who should be assisted in accepting this gift of God which the Church has received from her Lord and which by his grace she always safeguards."

The third principle is that the primary aim of formation is not to call out a candidate, or to detect their wrongdoing, but to assist the candidate to grow into an intimacy with Christ, the Incarnate Word. The immediate purpose of the formation of candidates is to introduce them to a life of consecration and assist them to become aware of its specific character within the Catholic Church. The primary aim of formation is to assist those who are discerning this divine call to consecrate their lives to God, and to realize their unity of life in Christ through His Spirit. Prior to the Second Vatican Council, the Church was concerned about the formation of consecrated men and women. That is why the Second Vatican Council gave doctrinal principles and general norms on formation of consecrated persons in the sixth Chapter of the dogmatic constitution, *Lumen Gentium*, and in the decree *Perfectae Caritatis*. The Code of Canon Law also indicates in a more precise way the norms and exigencies required for a suitable renewal of the formation process (# 641-661).

The fourth principle stated that the Holy Spirit is the Principal Formator. In this, the structures of a formation community, while ever remaining sufficiently clear and solid, will leave ample room for responsible initiatives and decisions guided by the inspiration of the Holy Spirit. The will of God is expressed most often and preeminently through the mediation of the Church and its magisterium. The witness of the elder members in a community has greater influence on the young than any other theoretical consideration. Thus, the formator or team of formators, through their life and experience, give witness to the presence and action of the Holy Spirit in the formation community. This helps the formator to be patient and to not be inclined to be totally in control of all that is happening. The Holy Spirit is the principal agent who brings transformative experience to the candidates/formatees.

The fifth principle emphasizes that the goal of formation is to offer the candidate a conducive atmosphere for nurturing his/her vocation: A spiritual atmosphere that includes an austerity of life and an apostolic enthusiasm, which are conducive to their following Christ according to the radicalism of their consecration. Thus, the emphasis is not to sort out the good from the bad! It is therefore always indispensable to keep drawing from the pedagogical experience of the Church all that can assist and enrich formation and place them in a community suitable for the individuals within it and for their religious or priestly vocation. What is being emphasized here is an atmosphere that helps the candidates to realize

Chapter 8: Attitudes and Dispositions

and maintain solitude and silence. This is highly recommended as indispensable during the whole time of initial formation.

The sixth principle stresses the responsibility of the Candidate for his or her own formation. It is the candidate who holds the first responsibility for saying "yes" to the call which has been received and for accepting all the consequences of this response. It is not primarily in the order of the intellect, but of the whole of life. The formator is therefore invited to be patient with the candidate and to allow the Holy Spirit to motivate the candidate to say "yes" to the divine invitation. This helps the formator to make proposals of the path of growth to the candidate and offer them as suggestions for the candidate to take them up and accept responsibility to put the proposed values into practice.

The seventh principle of incarnational formation points to the method of religious formation that strongly appeals to the conscience and personal responsibility of the candidate. This helps the candidate to internalize the values of consecrated life, and at the same time, the role of life which is proposed to them by the director of formation so that they may find within themselves the justification for their practical choices and find in the Holy Spirit their fundamental dynamism and vitality.

The eighth principle of formation emphasizes that a right balance between the group formation and individual formation should be maintained in such a manner that the uniqueness of each candidate is secured and facilitated. It will therefore be necessary to pay very close attention to each individual so that each advances at his or her own pace, and the content of formation and the way it is communicated are suitable to the one receiving it.

The ninth principle highlights that the role of a formator is that of facilitation and the Holy Spirit is the principal formator. The whole of the spiritual tradition of the Church attests to the decisive character of the role of formators for the success of the work of formation. Their role is to help the candidates to discern the authenticity of their call to religious life in the initial phase of formation, and to assist the candidates toward a successful personal dialogue with God while they are discovering the ways in which He seems to wish them to advance. The formators achieve this delicate responsibility through the process of the accompaniment of the candidate along the paths of the Lord by means of direct and regular dialogue, always respecting the proper role of the confessor and spiritual director in the strict sense of the words.

Furthermore, one of the main tasks of those responsible for formation is to ascertain whether the candidate is making effective use of spiritual direction. Formators should offer the candidates solid nourishment, both doctrinal and practical, always in keeping with their stage of formation. Formators should progressively examine and evaluate the progress that is being made by those in their charge, in light of the fruits of the Holy Spirit. They have the responsibility to decide whether the individual called has the capacities which are required at this time by the Magisterium, by the Local Church, and by the requirements of the religious institute.

On the side of the formator, the Church requires that in addition to a sound knowledge of Catholic faith and morals, those who are responsible for formation need to have psychological equilibrium and the human qualities of insight and responsiveness. Formators are also required to have a certain level of experiential

Chapter 8: Attitudes and Dispositions

knowledge of God and of prayer, wisdom resulting from attentive and prolonged listening to the word of God, love for the liturgy, and understanding of their role in spiritual and ecclesial formation. Some of the other attitudes and dispositions necessary for a person entrusted with the delicate ministry of formation include essential cultural competence, sufficient time, and good will to attend to the candidates individually and not just as a group. It is also emphasized that formators should inwardly possess and outwardly manifest inner serenity, availability, patience, understanding, and a genuine affection for those who have been confided to their pastoral responsibility.

The tenth principle is that the ministry of formation is collaborative in nature. If there is a group of formators under the personal responsibility of the one who is in charge of formation, the individual members should act in harmony, keenly aware of their common responsibility. Under the direction of the superior/Rector or the seminary, "they should cultivate the closest harmony of spirit and action" and should form with one another and with those in their charge, one united family. No less necessary is the cohesion and continued collaboration among those responsible for the different stages of formation.

It has been affirmed that the fruitfulness of the work of formation as a whole is the fruit of the collaboration between those responsible for formation and the candidates. Even when the candidates assume a large part of the responsibility for their own formation, this responsibility can still only be exercised fruitfully within a specific tradition, and with the facilitation of the formation team. This is made practical by the living example of collaboration and the cooperative spirit among the formators. These are some of the values of the Church, of which those responsible for formation are the witnesses and immediate advocates.

In the discernment and accompaniment of candidates, these principles lead to a realization of the commended attitudes for more effective incarnational formative experiences that result in the transformation of the candidates. These attitudes and dispositions include transparency, openness, and trust. They lead to the process of growth in self-awareness. Experience has also revealed that the most difficult and challenging aspect of religious formation is the accompaniment of the candidate.

It has been discovered that many religious priests find the process very challenging, even those who have psychological skills. Candidates view the process of accompaniment as a thing to avoid when possible. This leads one to ask: What could be the primary issue? There are four main factors we should consider: issues related to trust, openness, the level of transparency, and the grace of self-awareness. These are challenging realities in the formative process.

Let us consider *trust* as the main factor that facilitates authentic incarnational formative experiences. Do the candidates trust the formator, and does the formator feel trusted? If a formator does not feel trusted, the formator will not display dispositions and attitudes that facilitate growth in trust for the candidates. For instance, if you were to be appointed as a formator, would you feel trusted? Some people feel trusted when appointed as a formator, while others see it as a punishment. Once the formation work is

Chapter 8: Attitudes and Dispositions

perceived as a punishment by the formator, trust and development of the other three qualities of openness, transparency, and self-awareness become challenging realities in the formative process.

It is not uncommon that many religious people resist the ministry of formation for quite a few reasons, but trust is foundational to the effectiveness of the formative process. If a formator does not feel trusted in the first place, the foundation for formation and transformation is already destroyed. This echoes the value that we pray in Psalm 11:3: "If the foundations be destroyed, what can the just do?" If a formator feels trusted when appointed to the ministry, he or she will certainly bring that trust to the process of formation and more effectively facilitate the transformation of the candidates. Consequently, the candidates will perceive and live such trust.

The attitude and disposition that communicate trust are important indicators that could serve as criteria for a formator to evaluate if he or she is living an authentic life as a religious person and a formator. It is a basis for the formator to discern if the candidates trust him or her, and if they in return trust the candidates. It is by identifying concrete attitudes and dispositions that communicate trust that the formator can then use as indicators to feel that the candidates are honestly trusting and entrusting their lives to them, thus making it possible to guide them to a successful achievement of their goal of becoming truly devout religious. One of the key questions that a formator should ask themselves is: What would I do to assure the candidates that I am genuinely there for them to guide them to a successful formation journey?

The value of dispositions and attitudes that communicate trust is very foundational in the formative process because the candidates' experience of trust is one of the indicators that enables them to feel that the formator is authentic, to let go of their defenses, and to allow the Holy Spirit to transform them. To build such trust as an indicator of an authentic life, what the church, the religious institutes, and the candidates expect may be summarized in six key values:

1. Sincerity manifested in the ability to keep confidentiality;
2. Reliability manifested in respectful listening;
3. Commitment manifested by availability;
4. A life of Integrity manifested by prudent self-disclosure;
5. Competency manifested by the knowledge of charism and spirituality of the institute;
6. Consistency by not changing attitudes toward religious life and ministry.

A story is told of a man who approached three workers who were doing the same job. "What are you doing?" he asked each one of them separately and got different answers. "I am cutting the stones," replied the first. "I am earning my livelihood," replied the second. "I am building a Church," replied the third. Each of the three workers saw themselves as linked to a different purpose, each different from the others, although all worked alike and were engaged in the same task. Thus, the link we establish with our ministries has a lot to do with the effectiveness of it, be it in the area of formation ministry or other pastoral ministries.

Chapter 8: Attitudes and Dispositions

The degree of the incarnational formative experience and transformation that a formator facilitates for the candidate depends on the quality of the inner purpose in the heart of the formator. This serves as the spring-board from which the ministry is effectively implemented. It is from this springboard that the formator serves as a facilitator, with the awareness of the Holy Spirit as the principal formator.

Openness to the influence of the Holy Spirit is the second important attitude and disposition that serves as an indicator for a fruitful incarnational formative experience. Openness is described as both a capacity and willingness to share and receive information, ideas/vision, thoughts, and inspirations as fruits of prayer, as well as feelings, both negative and positive in a mature manner. Openness is also practically expressed in terms of the willingness to listen keenly and respectfully to others who are sharing their feelings. The Holy Spirit does not work in a vacuum. The influence of the Holy Spirit penetrates the life of individuals through the life witness of the formator as well as the experience of community living, involving both the members of the formation team and other candidates in formation. This is an invitation for each of the agents in the formative ministry to question the level of their openness in their encounters with others, and their willingness to share and to listen keenly to all in the formation community. It is because of this that openness is regarded as one of the foundational values for those who desire to become religious.

The level of openness to the Holy Spirit, in the ways described above, can be regarded as the key to the incarnational transformative experience of formation. The degree to which one can attain such a level of openness depends on a number of factors, and it differs from candidate to candidate, and from formator to formator. It takes into consideration the formation received from childhood, social context, difference in ambience, and the natural talents of each one. This invites us to keep in mind the saying that 'grace builds on nature'. Remember that candidates naturally model the openness of their formator.

It has been described as unfair if a formator truly discerns that a candidate is not suitable but continues to cover over this issue and not address it openly for fear of hurting the candidate. If a candidate is resisting formation from all indications, the formator should challenge him- or herself to be open and address it in a manner that helps the candidate to make a different decision sooner, rather than delaying it until the situation becomes complex. In line with this view, most of the experienced formators are of the opinion that openness is indispensable for an authentic process of formation and transformation, for both the candidate and the formator. If a formator recognizes that his or her level of openness in the ministry is not good enough, he or she needs to seek help in order to foster openness for more effective formation and transformation for him- or herself and for the candidates.

Therefore, a formator is expected to guide the candidate in a way that motivates him or her toward a deeper comprehension of his or her personal charism, lived in relationship with God and with others. Therefore, it is about the formator living an authentic life. This does not mean that the formator becomes an angel or impeccable. This would be expecting too much. The formator should recognize that he or she is an earthen jar containing very

Chapter 8: Attitudes and Dispositions

precious treasures. An authentic life would be more practical if the formator is just himself or herself and apologizes when things go wrong. This is one of the aspects of formation that make a good number of people resist the work of formation. They expect that they must be perfect and impeccable. However, what is truly needed is for the formator to be honest with him- or herself about his or her weaknesses and mistakes. This helps the formator to be open to the influence of the Holy Spirit. It is only then that the desired incarnational experience of the formation process manifests.

It can thus be concluded that these values, attitudes, and dispositions are the human components that God awaits from a person in order to enact the mystery of his divine action in the hearts. This implies that openness is a necessary background on which honest dialogue between the formators and candidates can happen. Openness creates a climate of confidence and trust between the formator and the candidate. It is so seriously foundational that it is suggested that if this is not possible, the candidate should be entrusted to another person with whom he or she will feel more at ease in being open and authentic. Open dialogues are indispensable not just for personal growth in becoming a religious person, but also for making a mature decision to leave the religious life, if necessary.

Chapter 9

Embodying The Love of the Incarnate Word in Mission

Sr. Adaku H. Ogbuji, CCVI

According to the Encyclopedia Britannica, the word mission is from a Latin word: *missio*, which is a translation of the Greek word *apostolē*. It literally means "a sending." A missionary is someone sent to evangelize. As Christians, our mission is to evangelize and be Jesus' witnesses, either with our words or our actions. "Preach the gospel at all times; and if necessary, use words," was attributed to St. Francis of Assisi. By virtue of our baptism, we are witnesses to the gospel and disciples of Jesus. To become evangelizers, we must first be evangelized. Some Christians do this in their families and societies, others in the parishes, some in religious communities, and many across nations. We usually think of a missionary as a baptized Christian, a priest, or a religious person who leaves home and goes to a foreign land to evangelize. Yes, but we are missionaries and evangelizers wherever we are! We are to live out our faith among the people with whom we live and those we serve.

When Jesus began his public ministry after his baptism, his first task was to preach about the kingdom of God and to witness to the love of God. As Jesus continued this mission, he chose disciples who would help him in the mission and would continue the mission after he had gone to heaven. He tried the capacity of his seventy-two disciples by sending them out on a mission without accompanying them (Lk. 10:1-23). They came back testifying what God did through them: "Lord, in your name, even the demons submit to us!" Jesus quickly cautioned them: "Do not rejoice that the spirits submit to you but rejoice that your names are written in heaven."

As Jesus continued to mentor his friends to whom he intended to hand over the mission of his Father, he said a powerful prayer for them as well as for those who would believe in Him through their preaching. Jesus prayed for all of us at this age and time and even those who would come after us. This was recorded in John's Gospel: "Father, as you have sent me into the world, so I have sent them into the world.... My prayer is not for them alone. I pray also for those who will believe in me through their message, that all of them may be one, Father, just as you are in me and I am in you. May they also be in us so that the world may believe that you have sent me" (John 17:18, 20–21).

Jesus did not stop at praying for the apostles; he handed over the mission to them through the "Great Commission," after his resurrection: "Go therefore, and make disciples of all nations, baptizing them in the name of the Father and of the Son and of the Holy Spirit, teaching them to observe all that I have commanded you; and behold, I am with you always, to the close of the age" (Matthew 28:19–20; *compare* Mark 16:15, Luke 24:47, John 20:21–22, and Acts 1:8). The disciples are not to proclaim what they like; they are Jesus' witnesses. They are to witness what they learned from the Master himself. They are to make disciples, too,

Chapter 9: Embodying the Love of the Incarnate Word in Mission 113

just like they were formed by Jesus. But before then, those whom they make disciples must truly encounter the Person of Jesus.

So many of them exhibited little faith even after the miracles of Jesus that Jesus was frustrated with them (Mk.6:30-53). Peter's true encounter with Jesus was at the Sea of Tiberias when the risen Lord asked him three times whether he loved him (Jn. 21:15-17). Thomas' encounter was when he put his hand on the side and hands of Jesus that were pierced through crucifixion, and he exclaimed "My Lord and my God!" Nathanael, also called Bartholomew, encountered the Lord when Philip introduced him to Jesus and Jesus said of him: "Here is a true child of Israel. There is no duplicity in him." And Nathanael responded, "How do you know me?" Jesus answered and said to him, "Before Philip called you, I saw you under the fig tree." Nathanael answered him, "Rabbi, you are the Son of God; you are the King of Israel." Jesus answered and said to him, "Do you believe because I told you that I saw you under the fig tree? You will see greater things than this. Amen, amen, I say to you, you will see heaven opened and the angels of God ascending and descending on the Son of Man" (Jn. 1:45-51).

Each of the disciples encountered the Lord in their respective and unique ways, and this encounter transformed their little faith; however, it didn't absolutely change who they thought Jesus was. For even after Jesus' resurrection, the disciples still didn't get it: "Lord, will you at this time restore the kingdom to Israel?" (Acts. 1:6).

Thus, the disciples were not to begin this mission until the Spirit of Jesus was sent to them. They needed the spirit of fortitude and wisdom, a counselor, and an advocate who would remind them of everything that Jesus taught them: "But the Counselor, the Holy Spirit, whom the Father will send in my name, he will teach you all things, and bring to your remembrance all that I have said to you" (Jn. 16:16, 26). Jesus even ordered the disciples never to leave Jerusalem until they received the Holy Spirit, the promise of the Father (Acts 1:4). After the descent of the Holy Spirit, the disciples began to witness the crucified Jesus, whom God raised from the dead (Acts 2:22-24). All these things point to the fact that "the Mission" is God's work which Jesus himself started and later sent his followers to continue. This mission continues today, and we are witnesses to Jesus' mission.

The Church exists for the mission of evangelization. And this mission is to live out the love of the Incarnate Word in our world, through our words and actions and in our relationships with people around us, as well as in our relationships with created things. However, it is imperative to have a relationship with the God of the mission. It is one thing to know about God. It is another to know God. How much do we know and love God? Do we know about God, or do we know God?

To know God is to have a deeper relationship with Him! The disciples know about Jesus. They know about the Hebrew Scriptures' prophecies! They also know about the coming of the Messiah! Peter even confessed that Jesus is the Christ. In other words, Jesus is the Messiah! But what followed immediately after this confession of faith was Jesus calling Peter Satan: "Get behind me Satan!" (Mt.16:13-23). Prior to this, Jesus was revealing what being a Messiah demands—-his death and resurrection. But Peter took him aside and began to rebuke him, saying, "God forbid it, Lord!

This must never happen to you." Jesus, then, rebuked Peter harshly by addressing him as Satan, who is a hindrance to him, and who sets his mind on human things rather than on divine things.

Peter was also found wanting when it came to defending Jesus, the Messiah! He denied Jesus, not once, but three times! We cannot carry out this mission without a deep relationship with God, whose mission we are called to do. This relationship is achieved through prayer, through reflecting on God's word, and through knowing God.

Jesus is our perfect role model; he demonstrated that prayer is an essential aspect of the mission. He would always take time to pray; "And after Jesus had dismissed the crowds, he went up on the mountain by himself to pray" (Mt. 14:23, Mk. 1:35). Before Jesus made important decisions in the mission, he would find time to pray. For instance, before he chose the twelve apostles (Lk. 6:12-13). He also taught the disciples how to pray as well as the importance of prayer (Mt.21:22; Mt. 18:19-20; Lk. 11:2-4). Even when the mission became very challenging, Jesus never ceased to seek God's will. He prayed in the Garden of Gethsemane (Mt. 26:36-56) before his arrest. In the same way, we cannot embark on this mission successfully without the power of prayer. Prayer connects us with the Incarnate Word and helps us to enter a deeper relationship with God.

I want to believe that every missionary has a personal encounter and relationship with the Lord through prayer because we cannot preach about Jesus if we do not believe in him or love him (Rm. 10:12-15). When was your first encounter with Jesus Christ, that encounter that filled you with joy? We all have experienced Jesus in a personal way! We have to be in a deeper relationship with the Lord before we can share that experience with others. Through prayer, we encounter Jesus just as Peter, Andrew, James, and John encountered him by the Sea of Galilee (Mt. 4:18-22) and immediately left everything, including their family and occupation and followed him, even with their little faith and not fully comprehending the mission. Pope Francis called our first encounter with Jesus the "first Galilee encounter" in line with the call and transformation of the first four disciples of Jesus (Pope Francis "Return to the First Galilee," morning meditation in the chapel of the Domus Sanctae Marthae on February 7, 2014).

This encounter is incarnational! The Word of God, Jesus Christ himself, finds a dwelling place in each of us. We embody his love, then we share that love generously with others in a missionary spirit. It is impossible to embody the love of the Incarnate Word and live a wayward life. Of course, we are not immune to sinning, but we always have to make the effort to return to our first Love—Jesus Christ. Do you still remember your first Galilee encounter as a missionary? How often do you revisit this space in prayer, especially when the mission is challenging?

I still remember with nostalgia when I left Nigeria in 2004 for the first time to seek God's will for me in religious life in Kenya. I was beaming with joy and love for the Incarnate Word; at the same time, I had mixed feelings of anxiety and fear of how I would be received. On arrival, I found Sr. Francesca Kearns waiting for me. She was the Vocation Director for our Congregation in Kenya then. My joy knew no bounds as I experienced her hospitality and

Chapter 9: Embodying the Love of the Incarnate Word in Mission

care. Welcoming a missionary in a foreign land, in a spirit of compassion, is very crucial. In some places, the missionaries are not welcomed.

I recall the experience of our founder, Bishop Claude Marie Dubuis, the second bishop of the then-Diocese of Galveston, when he arrived in Castroville, Texas. The people were unfriendly and hostile to him, but with great trust in God and devotion to Mother Mary, with his witty and humorous attitude, he began to win them over. On one of his evangelizing trips, he was attacked and captured by a group of Comanches (Native Americans). He introduced himself as a "Captain of the Great Spirit." He was immediately released and saluted (Sister M. Consuelo Coffey, 1983, *The Dubuis Family Papers, 1846-1895*).

As they served in the mission and evangelized, Fr. Dubuis and his friend Fr. M. Chazelle built a small church and their home. They opened a school where they taught up to eighty children. Extreme poverty, hardship, and the challenges of an epidemic—cholera— and later the death of Fr. Chazelle, did not deter Fr. Dubuis from being a zealous missionary, even without enough financial resources. He wrote to his mother: "I do not have a penny—only the bounty of Divine Providence."

When the small church could no longer contain the faithful who were increasing in numbers, he and his new companion, Fr. Domenech, began to construct a bigger church. He was a pastor, a teacher, and a mason. One day, an Irish traveler asked a mason he saw where to find Fr. Dubuis. This mason walked over to a bucket of water, washed his hands and face, and replied: "Here I am!" The confused visitor was astounded and made a donation of ten piasters to his mission (Sister M. Consuelo Coffey, 1983, *The Dubuis Family Papers, 1846-1895*).

Our founder cared for the poor. He gave the kids of Castroville an education even when their parents could not afford the cost. As the second bishop of the then-Diocese of Galveston, his compassionate heart and courage would move him to seek and establish congregations of devout religious women who would attain to the suffering Jesus' in his diocese. Despite all the challenges he faced, I can confidently say that his missionary zeal and personal spirituality were ingrained in incarnational spirituality which is the basis of our spirituality today.

A missionary life without challenges would be like going to school without lessons to learn. Challenges come in the mission not to depress or get us down, but to make us stronger and help us to grow. To be a missionary is to carry a cross, to go the extra mile to serve. Jesus did not promise a cross-free discipleship; he rather promised to be with us (Mt. 28:20; Luke 9:23). Some crosses are heavy, others seem light. But if we try to run away from the challenges of being a missionary, be assured that you will run into another just like it, although it may have a different face or name. A wise saying has it that "we can never lose anything that belongs to us, nor can we possess what is not really ours." In being missionaries, we lose our lives to gain them in Christ (Lk. 14:26). The consolation is that the will of God will not take us where His grace will not sustain us. St. Paul puts it well: "God's grace is always enough for us and His power is made perfect in weakness" (2 Cor. 12:7-10).

Chapter 9: Embodying the Love of the Incarnate Word in Mission

In God's loving plan for us, no burden can fall upon us before we are given the grace and strength to meet them. Pope Francis encourages us to always return to that first encounter with the Lord in the face of challenges. According to Pope Francis, "The secret of joy and perseverance (in the mission) is to go there, to return to our first Galilee, where we encounter the Lord again and again, on which He must increase and we must decrease" (Pope Francis, 2014, Return to the First Galilee). It takes humility and prayer to allow Jesus to increase, while we decrease, like John the Baptist. Sometimes, our inflated ego gets in the way, and we want to claim the glory, or we think the mission is ours! The mission is God's! We are only workers in God's vineyard!

Similarly, consecrated life is for the mission of evangelization. Being set aside for God does not exist without mission. We are required to leave the center and travel toward the margins of society to be the healing hands and feet of Jesus. In embodying the love of the Incarnate Word in mission, we go beyond and out of our comfort zones to the areas in society that challenge us and invite us to be witnesses to God's love and compassion. In his letter to his parents on June 6, 1846, Bishop Dubuis, our Founder, expressed his taste of suffering that is embedded in being a missionary. He wrote: "I am going to tell you about the most dangerous animal. It is not the crocodile; he devours promptly…It is not the bear; he is cowardly. The most dangerous animal is the mosquito. He lives only twenty-four hours, but he has wrought on me the most appalling ravages: my head, arms, legs, and my entire body is covered with its bites and there is severe swelling all over. At times they swarm about me by the hundreds; yet were they numbered in the millions, I could not regret being a missionary" (Sister M. Consuelo Coffey, 1983, *The Dubuis Family Papers, 1846-1895*).

With this touching letter of our founder, I have asked myself several questions over and over again. Is there an experience that will make me regret being a missionary? When the challenges of being a missionary come, will I still have the joy and burning zeal that I experienced during my first Galilee encounter? How am I embodying the love of the Incarnate Word in mission? What legacy am I leaving behind? When my eulogy is read at my funeral, would I feel proud of how I had spent my life as a missionary?

As a Church, we have embarked on a synodal journey that will last from the year 2021 to 2023. And this process has a deeper missionary dimension, intended to enable the Church to better witness to the Gospel, especially with those who live on the spiritual, social, economic, political, geographical, and existential peripheries of our world. The synodality process calls us to walk together as a family of God's household. We are called as a Church to journey together, to inspire trust, to bind up wounds, to allow hope to flourish, and to weave together relationships. We are a missionary Church whose doors should be open. Pope Francis explains it well: "Our churches' doors should always be open, so that if someone, moved by the Spirit, comes there looking for God, he or she will not find a closed door" (*The Joy of the Gospel*, no.47).

Sometimes, our doors are more open only to those who are rich, or who are of the same race, class, or tribe as us. We treat the poor with disdain as recorded in the letter of St. James (2:1-9). Bishop Romero once said: "A Church which is not united with the poor and does not denounce from the perspective of the poor, the injustices committed against them, is not the true Church of Jesus Christ."

We are called to be where the cry of the poor meets the ear of God. We are to listen to the cry of the poor, defend them, and have a love of preference for the poor. Pope Francis laments in *Evangelii Gaudium* that too many Christians are living and "acting as if God did not exist, making decisions as if the poor did not exist, setting goals as if others did not exist, working as if people, who have not received the Gospel, did not exist" (no. 80). What is the poor crying for today? Are we aware of them? To embody the love of the Incarnate Word in mission, we must follow the Master—Jesus Christ—whose option is for the poor and sinners. He defended the defenseless and released those in bondage. He brought hope to the hopeless, relief to the oppressed, and forgiveness to sinners.

As missionaries, we must evangelize to both the oppressor and the oppressed. To the oppressor, we must speak a message of criticism and a challenge to conversion, and to the oppressed, we must speak a message of peace and hope. That is what the Master did! He condemned the atrocities of the religious leaders of his time, who were oppressing the poor, and he gave hope and love to the oppressed. The words of Pope Francis summarize the need to go out and evangelize:

> "I prefer a Church which is bruised, hurting, and dirty because it has been out on the streets, rather than a Church which is unhealthy from being confined and from clinging to its own security. I do not want a Church concerned with being at the center and then ends by being caught up in a

web of obsessions and procedures. If something should rightly disturb us and trouble our consciences, it is the fact that so many of our brothers and sisters are living without the strength, light, and consolation born of friendship with Jesus Christ, without a community of faith to support them, without meaning and a goal in life. More than by fear of going astray, my hope is that we will be moved by the fear of remaining shut up within structures which give us a false sense of security, within rules which make us harsh judges, within habits which make us feel safe, while at our door people are starving and Jesus does not tire of saying to us: 'Give them something to eat'" (Mk. 6:37) (*Evangelii Gaudium*, no. 49).

The missionary's spirit of an option/preference for the poor and of embodying the love of the Incarnate Word in mission demand that the missionaries remove their "sandals" (ethnocentric attitude, bias, prejudices, and myopic lens) as they enter the mission land or as they encounter the "other." Incarnational spirituality changes the missionary's practice and allows the missionary to enter the garden of the host with respect, dialogue, and vulnerability. In this way, the missionaries are aware that God was already with the people before their arrival and treat them with love that is flowing from the Incarnate Word.

This approach is different from the colonial mentality that was used to evangelize the mission land, especially in African countries, from the 18th to 20th centuries. For these missionaries, there was no faith in God in the new conquered land. Therefore, faith in the true God had to be implanted in the local people. Assimilation was used instead of adaptation. St. Paul used adaptation when he was preaching to the people of Athens: "Men of Athens, I perceived that in every way, you are very religious. For as I passed along, and observed the objects of your worship, I also found an altar with an inscription, 'to an unknown god.' What therefore you worship as unknown, this I proclaim to you" (Acts. 17:22-23). Paul did not condemn them for worshipping several gods. He rather used what they were familiar with to bring them to the one true God.

The consequence of using assimilation in African countries was that the local people accepted the God of the missionary, but still consulted their God that was condemned by the missionaries, thus continuing their way of worship. That is why Christianity did not take proper root in some African countries. Many Christians went to church on Sunday to please the missionaries, and at night, they worshiped the God of their ancestors that was handed down to them. On another note, the missionaries were passionate to welcome Africans to the Church, however, most European religious congregations were unwilling to accept Africans as full members. The constant justification was that Africans were not culturally disposed to the demands of religious life. This gave rise to the formation of religious congregations for Africans.

Evangelization is the mission of the church. It must be done with the compassion that is flowing from the heart of the Incarnate Word. Pope Paul VI affirmed this in his letter on Evangelization in the Modern World:

> We wish to confirm once more that the task of evangelizing all people constitutes the essential mission of the Church. It is a task and mission which the vast and profound changes of present day society make all the more urgent. Evangelizing is in fact the grace and vocation proper to the Church, her deepest identity. She exists in order to evangelize. (Pope Paul VI, 1975, *Evangelii Nuntiandi*, no. 14)

Evangelization must be done with sensitivity, freedom, and love. "We are called in freedom," St. Paul says. "But we do not use this freedom as an opportunity for the flesh; but rather, to serve one another through love. For the whole law is fulfilled in one statement, namely, 'You shall love your neighbor as yourself.' But if you go on biting and devouring one another, beware that you are not consumed by one another" (Gal. 5: 13-15). When missionaries embody the love of the Incarnate Word in their mission, there will be freedom and selfless compassionate services. If not, then we are going to bite and devour each other, and we will be consumed by lack of love.

Our Mission is to evangelize! Our mission is to preach, with our actions first, and, if necessary, with our words. We are called to walk the talk! It will be hypocritical or pharisaic if we preach one thing and do another. As disciples and witnesses, we are called to daily conversion. We are called to serve one another in love, and we do it wherever we are missioned. As missionaries, we are on a journey, Synodal walk! We are reminded to walk together, and not to leave anyone behind. However, it is still a personal journey, and at the end of the journey, we will all give an account of how much we have loved.

At this time, I am asking you the same questions I asked myself above: When your eulogy is read at your funeral, will you be proud of how you had spent your life as a missionary? What legacy are you leaving behind? Is there an experience that will make you regret being a missionary? When the challenges of being a missionary come, will you still have the joy and burning zeal that you experienced during your first Galilee encounter? How are you embodying the love of the Incarnate Word today in the mission? Jesus is still commanding us to: "Go and make disciples of all nations, baptizing them in the name of the Father, and of the Son, and of the Holy Spirit." May God grant us the grace to listen and respond like Mary and the Psalmist: "Here I am Lord, I come to do your will" (Ps. 40:6-10; Heb. 10:9; Lk. 1:38).

REFERENCES:

Coffey, C. (1983). The Dubuis Family Papers, 1846-1895).

Pope Francis. (2013). *Evangelii Gaudium* (*The Joy of the Gospel*). Accessed from https://www.vatican.va/content/francesco/en/apost_exhortations/documents/papa-francesco_esortazione-ap_ 20131124_evangelii-gaudium.html.

Pope Francis. (2014). "Return to the First Galilee," A morning meditation in the chapel of the Domus Sanctae Marthae. Accessed from https://www.vatican.va/content/francesco/en/cotidie/2014/documents/papa-francesco-cotidie_20140207_first-galilee.html.

Pope Paul VI. (1975). *Evangelii Nuntiandi.* Accessed from https://www.vatican.va/content/paul-vi/en/apost_exhortations/documents/hf_p-vi_exh_19751208_evangelii-nuntiandi.html

Chapter 10

Embodying the Love of the Incarnate Word

Sr. Adaku H. Ogbuji, CCVI

Incarnational Spirituality sees our incarnate or embodied state as sacred. In our bodies, we celebrate our physical nature as well as our embodied spiritual nature. In doing so, we value and respect each individual's life. We subsequently live out our Incarnational life by our intentional acts of love. When we allow ourselves to care for ourselves and others, it refills the heart, energizes the body, and nourishes the soul. In that moment of opening our hearts to self and others, we recognize the immense healing power of compassion, forgiveness, and reconnection with life and love.

Apparently, we don't know how to love because we are "a work in progress." Our love is conditioned and sometimes not selfless. But Jesus, the Incarnate Word, is molding us to love as he loves, in selflessness, through sacrifice, and in an incarnational way. To love is to sacrifice and to be selfless in relationship! Sometimes, we find the molding of Jesus a little bit harsh and too demanding! The Potter—Jesus (Jer. 18:1-11)—is trying to mold us like him, but we complain sometimes of either too much heat, too much pruning, or too much sacrifice. It reminded me of the story of a teacup; the author is unknown.

A story is told of a couple who used to go to England to shop at a beautiful antique store. This particular trip was to celebrate their 25th wedding anniversary. They both liked antiques and pottery, and especially teacups, and so spotting an exceptional cup they asked, "May we see that? We've never seen a cup quite so beautiful."

As the lady at the antique store handed the cup to them, suddenly the teacup spoke. "You don't understand." It said, "I have not always been a teacup. There was a time when I was just a lump of red clay. My master took me and rolled me, pounded, and patted me over and over and I yelled out, 'Don't do that. I don't like it. Leave me alone!' But he only smiled gently and said, 'Not yet!'"

"Then, I was placed on a spinning wheel and suddenly I was spun around and around, 'Stop it! I'm getting so dizzy! I'm getting so dizzy! I'm going to be sick!' I screamed. But the master said, quietly; 'Not yet!'"

"He spun me and poked and prodded and beat me out of shape to suit himself and then he put me in the oven. I never felt such heat. I yelled and knocked and pounded at the door. 'Help! Get me out of here!' I could see him through the opening, and I could read his lips as he shook his head from side to side, 'Not yet!'"

"When I thought I couldn't bear it another minute, the door opened. He carefully took me out and put me on the shelf, and I began to cool. 'Oh, that felt so good! Ah, this is much better,' I thought. But after I cooled, he picked me up and he brushed and painted me all over. The fumes were horrible. I thought I would gag. 'Oh, please, stop it! Stop it!' I cried. He only shook his head and said: 'Not yet!'"

"Then suddenly he put me back into the oven. Only it was not like the first time. This time it was twice as hot and I just knew I would suffocate. I begged… I pleaded… I screamed. I cried. I was convinced I would never make it. I was ready to give up and just then the door opened, and he took me out and again placed me on the shelf where I cooled and waited, wondering: 'What is he going to do with me next?'"

"An hour later he handed me a mirror and said, 'Look at yourself.' And I did. I said, 'That's not me, that couldn't be me. It's beautiful. I'm beautiful!' Quietly, he spoke: 'I want you to remember,' he said, 'I know it hurt to be rolled and pounded and patted, but had I just left you alone, you'd have dried up. I know it made you dizzy to spin around on the wheel, but if I had stopped, you would have crumbled. I know it hurt and it was hot and disagreeable in the oven, but if I hadn't done that, you never would have hardened. You would not have had any color in your life, if I had not painted you. And if I hadn't put you back in that second oven, you wouldn't have survived for long because your hardness would not have been held together. Now you are a finished product! Now you are what I had in mind when I first began working with you.'"
(https://www.creativebiblestudy.com/teacup-story.html).

Conclusion

God knows what He is doing with us. God is the potter, and we are the clay. He will mold us and fashion us, if we allow Him, into a flawless piece of work, to love like Him, forgive like Him, and be merciful like Him. We will thus become more incarnational, more human and more loving! And when life seems too hard to bear or we feel like we are in a fiery furnace of trials, we will still embody the love of the Incarnate Word.

We embody the love of the Incarnate Word when we:

- Become altruistic. We move beyond our comfort zones and help others, especially those who will not return the favor. We sacrifice for them and share our gifts with gladness and love, not expecting anything in return and not out of duty. Altruistic behavior actually improves the self-esteem and well-being of the giver.
- Avoid judgment: It is funny that sometimes we assume that we know the intention of others and we judge them by their behavior. Other times, we assume that others need to figure out what we intended! Intention is invisible! When we assume that we know people's intentions by their behavior and especially when we do not communicate our needs and intention; then, we give others the permission to assign meaning, belief, and draw conclusions to what is said. Be curious! Don't judge or assume!

- Become sensitive to the needs of people around us; we become more empathetic and try to put ourselves in the shoes of those around us and their hurts.
- Provide affection, emotional warmth, and unconditional love to people around us. The good thing about practicing these virtues is that you receive them back. The Scripture says: "The more you give, the more you will receive" (Pro. 11:24-31).
- Practice gratitude: "Gratitude is the best attitude," says a popular adage. When we reflect on the goodness of God and the things in our life that we were given without merit, we cannot but make gratitude our attitude.
- Become kind to self: Sometimes, we are our own worst enemies and not kind to ourselves. It is crucial to know that we are fallen human beings with wounds and flaws, and we make mistakes daily. Ruminating on our flaws and defects brings self-loathing, self-doubt, hopelessness, self-hatred, self-disgust, self-pity, pessimism, jealousy, and causes us to compare ourselves with others whom we think are better. These are unkind behaviors to self! A pessimistic attitude serves no benefit to you or to anyone around you; rather, it makes you a bitter person with a negative energy. No one likes to swim in pessimism, except those who are cynical, and exhibit a negative attitude and outlook. Instead, practice self-forgiveness and compassion to move forward in a more positive way. These attitudes are important for self-care and self-love!

Compassion and forgiveness toward self and those who hurt us help us to be free from unnecessary stress and anxiety. Stories of connection, love, and kindness are literally roadmaps to peace. And we should tell these stories often, just like the stories of our salvation history. As Christians, we celebrate and recount the story of the incarnation of Jesus and rejoice not only in his divinity but also in his humanity. In telling our stories, we are called to imitate Christ by our own daily incarnating activities and historical narrations. Yes! Just as Jesus became a human being and lived humanely and compassionately, each human person is to help make the world a better place, even if it is a drop in the ocean. Of course, without this drop the ocean is incomplete. We, like Jesus, are incarnational people—people of the spirit and of the flesh. And just as Jesus integrated his flesh and his spirit in compassionate services, we are called to imitate him to make this world a better place.

It is not enough to stay in the chapel praying! We have to incarnate our prayer with compassionate service and become the hands and feet of Jesus to those we live and work with. As explained above, "If something should rightly disturb us and trouble our consciences, it is the fact that so many of our brothers and sisters are living without the strength, light and consolation born of friendship with Jesus Christ, without a community of faith to support them, without meaning and a goal in life" (*Gaudium Evangelii*, no. 49). We need to have a heart of flesh and reach out to those in need in our communities and in our ministries. We have to allow Jesus to take flesh in our relationship with one another and in our way of serving others. Mahatma Gandhi expressed it this way, "In prayer it is better to have a heart without words than

Chapter 10: Embodying the Love of the Incarnate Word

words without a heart." We feel at home and very comfortable when we are approached in a compassionate way and with people who are more compassionate, but we are threatened and unsafe when the reverse is true. If we love to be treated in a compassionate way, why is it hard for us to treat others as we would love to be treated?

Just imagine you are sick and a nurse/doctor enters your room with a good smile and asks after your welfare in a kind-hearted way. This will foster a quick recovery and make the pain more bearable. Just imagine the reverse! So, why is it hard for us to practice the golden rule? (Mt. 7:12.). When we reach out to others in need and show them kindness, we give them a reason to believe in the goodness of humanity. We therefore are embodying the love of the Incarnate Word as He commanded: "Be compassionate just as your Father is compassionate. Don't judge, and you won't be judged. Don't condemn, and you won't be condemned. Forgive, and you will be forgiven. Give, and it will be given to you. A good portion—packed down, firmly shaken, and overflowing—will fall into your lap. The portion you give will determine the portion you receive in return" (Lk. 6:36-38).

I will leave us with a quote from Wayne W. Dyer: "If you have the choice between being right and being kind, choose being kind, and you will always be right!" Let us choose compassion and kindness, and we will become incarnate persons who embody the love of Jesus, the Incarnate Word to those around us and in our world!

References

Brocard, S. (1970). *The Vatican Oracle.* California: Duckworth Pub.

Catholic Update. (2022). "What Did Jesus Mean? Unpacking Gospel Revelations." Accessed from https://www.liguori.org/.

Doherty, C. (1995). *The Gospel Without Compromise.* Ontario, Canada: Madonna House Publications.

Fournée, J. (2000). *Praying the Angelus.* New York: Crossroad Publishing Company.

Garcia, E. D. (2021). Presidential Address: Creating Space for the Future: Cutting Deeper Grooves of Transforming Love into Evolution. 2021 Virtual Assembly of the Leadership Conference of Women Religious (LCWR), August 11-13th.

Garvin, M. P. (2021). *Intergenerational Living: "From Generation to Generation.* Lecture Notes for the Religious Formation Conference, November 2021 Congress.

Gittings, A. J. (2015). *Living Mission Interculturally: Faith, Culture, and the Renewal of Praxis.* Collegeville, MN: Liturgical Press.

Kornfield, J. (2011). "The Ancient Heart of Forgiveness." *Mind and Soul Magazine.* Accessed from https://greatergood.berkeley.edu/article/item/the_ancient_heart_of_forgiveness.

Lacey P. A. & Dewey A, Eds. (2013). *The Collected Poems of Denise Levertov.* New York: New Directions.

Lesher, M. (2018). The Passion of Youth Meets the Wisdom of Age. *VISION: A Resource of the National Religious Vocation Conference.* Accessed from https://vocationnetwork.org/en/articles/show/605-the-passion-of-youth-meets-the-wisdom-of-age

Lewis, C. S. (1949). *The Weight of Glory and Other Addresses.* New York: Macmillan Company.

McBrien, R, (2012). Pope John XXIII's Opening Address to the Second Vatican Council. Accessed from https://www.ncronline.org/blogs/essays-theology/pope-john-xxiiis-opening-address-second-vatican-council.

Montana, S. (2018). Why Forgiveness is Worth It. Accessed from https://www.ted.com/talks/sarah_montana_why_forgiveness_is_worth_it?language=en

Motivational Stories. Accessed from http://assets.ngin.com/attachments/document/0040/1426/Motivational_Stories.pdf

Nicholas, K. (2021). *Under the Sky we Make: How to Be Human in a Warming World.* New York: G.P. Putnam's Sons.

O'Brien, S. (2002). *Walking With our Ancestors: Ignatian Exercises with the Mother of Jesus and Mary Ward Spirituality.* Nairobi, Kenya. Paulines Publications Africa.

Ogbuji A. H. (2019). *Influence of Childhood Experiences on Faith Development: A Journey Towards Wholeness.* Umuahia, Nigeria: Lumen Press.

Ogbuji, A. H. (2021). *Out of the Lips of Infants, Wisdom Comes: Retelling the Bible Stories.* Nairobi, Kenya: Franciscan Kolbe Press.

Pope Francis (2015). *Laudato Si'*- Encyclical Letter on Care for our Common Home, §159.

Pope Francis. (2013). *Evangelii Gaudium* (The Joy of the Gospel) Accessed from https://www.vatican.va/content/francesco/en/apost_exhortations/documents/papa-francesco_esortazione-ap_20131124_evangelii-gaudium.html.

Pope Francis (2017). TED Talk "Why the Only Future Worth Building Includes everyone." Accessed from https://www.ted.com/talks/his_holiness_pope_francis_why_the_only_future_ worth_building_includes_everyone

Pope John Paul II. (1996). *Vita Consecrata*. Accessed from https://www.vatican.va/content/john-paul-ii/en/apost_exhortations/documents/hf_jp-ii_exh_25031996_vita-consecrata.html.

Rohr, R. (2018). *Creation Is the Body of God*. Accessed from https://cac.org/creation-is-the-body-of-god-2018-02-19/

Rohr, R. (1999). *The Holy Longing: The Search for a Christian Spirituality*. New York: Doubleday.

Santa, T. M. (2010, December). Incarnational Spirituality, *Scrupulous Anonymous* Vol. 47, No. 12 http://scrupulousanonymous.org/wp-content/uploads/2015/12/SA_1210.pdf

Singapore Christian. Accessed from https://www.singaporechristian.com.

Shore-Goss, R. E. (2016). *God is Green: An Eco Spirituality of Incarnate Compassion*. Eugene, OR: Cascade Books.

About the Contributors

Sister Margaret Bulmer, CCVI, was born and raised in Dublin, Ireland. She joined the Sisters of Charity of the Incarnate Word of Houston, Texas in 1954. She is a Nurse by profession and spent many years ministering in the Congregation's hospitals and clinics, serving the poor and uninsured. Most recently, her ministry was Director of Social Concerns for the Congregation. She is now retired but continues a part-time ministry of Community Outreach in the Congregation's St. Austin Center, Houston. Her motto has always been to "Serve Jesus Christ by ministering to those most in need."

Fr. Remigius Okonkwo Ikpe, OCD, PhD, is from the Nigerian Region of the Anglo-Irish Province of the Discalced Carmelite Order. He holds a Diploma in Philosophy; BA in Religious Studies; and Licentiate in Theology with specialization in Spiritual Theology. He also holds a master's degree in education and in psychology and a PhD in Education Management and in Spiritual Theology. He was the Director of the Institute of Spirituality and Religious Formation in Tangaza University College, Nairobi, Kenya. At present, he is the Prior of their community at Tabor Carmelite, Onuiyi, Nsukka, Nigeria.

Sister Adaku Helen (Helena) Ogbuji, CCVI, PhD, belongs to the Congregation of the Sisters of Charity of the Incarnate Word,

Houston, Texas. She is an author of several books: *Dealing Effectively with Domestic Abuse: The Ministry of Reconciliation and Healing*; *Influence of Childhood Experiences on Faith Development: A Journey Towards Wholeness*; and most recently, *Out of the Lips Of Infants, Wisdom Comes: Retelling The Bible Stories*. Her first degree was in Political Science and Public Administration. She holds a master's degree in theology, divinity, and psychology, and her PhD is in counselling psychology. She is presently the Formation Director and the Novice Director in their formation house in St. Louis, Missouri, USA.

Sister Patience S. Payne, SHF is from Liberia, West Africa, and a member of the Sisters of the Holy Family Liberia. She is a Social Worker and presently she is serving as the Novice Director of her Congregation as well as a social worker for St. Francis High School in the Diocese of Cape Palmas, Liberia.

www.ingramcontent.com/pod-product-compliance
Lightning Source LLC
LaVergne TN
LVHW020933090426
835512LV00020B/3331